Everything COLLEGE DIDN'T TEACH YOU ABOUT MONEY

Everything
COLLEGE
DIDN'T
TEACH
YOU
ABOUT
MONEY

BETH BROPHY

St. Martin's Press
New York

Design by Paolo Pepe

Library of Congress Cataloging in Publication Data

Brophy, Beth.
    Everything college didn't teach you about money.

    1. Finance, Personal.   2. College graduates—Finance,
Personal.   I. Title.
HG179.B746 1985   332.024   85–1718
ISBN 0-312-27234-0

First Edition

10 9 8 7 6 5 4 3 2 1

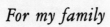
For my family

ACKNOWLEDGMENTS

Many people graciously shared their time, expertise, and personal experiences with me during the researching and writing of this book. I would like to thank everyone who helped me, especially:

Alexandra Armstrong, Larry Biehl, Betsy Bauer, Carol Bloomberg, Taylor Buckley, Ellen Dinoff, Richard Eisenberg, Karen Ferguson, Jerry Flint, Bob Garfield, Bill Giese, Susan Gordon, Richard Gumbiner, Steve Holub, Barbara Inkellis, Peter Miller, Joe Mintz, Wayne Nelson, and Elizabeth Sporkin.

Special thanks to:

Philippa Brophy, my sister and agent;

Tom Petruno, for his friendship and personal finance advice;

Arthur Karlin, for his advice, vision, and encouragement.

Some of the material appeared in a different form in *USA Today*.

CONTENTS

INTRODUCTION

You spent all those years getting that degree and the job's not bad. But you can't help wondering why, with all your education and all your professional skills, you're so dumb about money.

Alas, all those years of studying weren't enough. They taught you how to think but not whether to buy or rent, or how to tell the difference between being able to earn it and being able to keep it. Or how to make money work for you. So you emerge into the workplace lacking the essentials that guarantee a prosperous future: financial savvy and the discipline to build your resources.

Most important, the world of money has changed dramatically while you were cramming for the last psych exam. Sears is selling stocks, banks are marketing investment funds. What does it mean? It means there are sharks out there waiting to steal your money.

This is a book about financial self-defense. You must learn to protect and build what you have. You won't learn about leveraged buy-outs here. This is Money 101:

- How to save it before you lose it.
- Buy or rent a home; live alone or with a roommate.
- How to request and get a loan.
- Preparing for taxes and reducing your tax liability.

You can ignore these issues. You can sit in your little studio apartment, in your 30 to 40 percent tax bracket, and wonder why men and women with no better education than you and no better jobs are going to Aspen to ski and Club Med to swim.

But ignoring your money problems won't make them disappear. And this book can teach you how to master your financial future.

This book deals with the money problems facing young professionals by looking at seven people with different careers, habits, and attitudes about money. Three are single, one couple lives together, another couple is married.

Rachel, 25, landed a job in a mid-sized law firm in the Midwest. She earns $25,000 a year, much of which she spends in the clothing departments of Carson's and Hudson's. Another large percentage of that $25,000 is spent on Cuisinarts and Blue Mountain Coffee (from Jamaica, $20 a pound but delicious). Rachel is also into decorating (she just bought a signed Erté print for $1,025). You can see Rachel's problem: she spends a third of her income on clothes, a third on what-nots, and a third on her apartment.

Tom, 28, is an associate producer at a television station in the West. Alas, it isn't Boulder, but maybe some day. He makes $20,000, which is pretty good in Idaho. Unfortunately, they come and they go in this business. Unfortunately also, the station manager just mentioned that his wife's younger brother, Harold Twit, Jr., has graduated from Babson and will be coming out to look around next month. Tom knows this could mean résumé time again. How's his financial situation? Well, his spending patterns are erratic. He's too cheap to buy furniture, so he sleeps on a futon and eats standing up. But there's a $3,500 Pioneer stereo system in his nearly empty apartment.

Roy, 31, a third-year medical resident, is nearing the end of his training. Don't worry about him. He is already earning $40,000 as an ophthalmology resident (including moonlighting at the hospital). Roy plans on joining a private practice next year and within a couple of years should be earning well into the six figures. But he also knows that he will be at the top of the list passed from generation to generation of fast-talking tax shelter con men. As his earnings increase, so will his troubles, unless he learns a few things.

Ellen, 23, is an editorial assistant at a large publishing house in New York City. She loves her job except for her $13,500-a-year slave wage, which covers rent, subway fare, and panty hose. Her mother bought her a winter coat last year.

Worse, Ellen lives with her boyfriend Scott, 24, a graduate student in philosophy, who earns $10,000 as a teaching assistant while he finishes his Ph.D. Scott's mind is usually on weighty matters, which is fine, but he hasn't mastered the mundane details of daily life, such as paying the utility bill. Scott's lack of financial acumen leaves Ellen shouldering a heavy burden—one that she's not always equipped to handle properly.

Sue and Paul, married, seem to be in an enviable financial position. She, 27, has an MBA and earns $35,000 as a management consultant. Paul, 32, is an engineering manager at High Tech Chips Corp., at $45,000. But it's all salary—not a penny evades Mr. Tax Collector. They keep 65 cents on every new dollar earned, after federal, state, and local taxes. They want a baby before Sue is 37, but to give up her income, even for a few years, would be a disaster—especially with the bills they've run up.

Rachel, Tom, Roy, Ellen and Scott, and Sue and Paul are not alike, but they share a common goal with other busy young professionals: making money and keeping it.

Whatever your short-term and long-term financial goals—establishing a savings cushion, buying your first home, providing for children—achieving them requires accumulating capital. In this book, you, along with the characters introduced above, will learn how to do the following:

• Set up a comprehensive system for controlling expenses, paying bills, maintaining records, and saving.
• Figure your marginal tax bracket, hire a tax professional, achieve tax savings, and survive an audit.

- Buy the life, health, disability, and homeowner's and automobile policies that you need at the lowest cost.
- Establish and use credit and handle loan decisions.
- Devise and implement an investment strategy based on the risks and returns of stocks, bonds, and money market investments.
- Analyze whether to rent or buy a home and choose the best financing for your first home purchase.
- Select a first-rate team of financial counselors from the hordes of eager stockbrokers, accountants, lawyers, and financial planners.
- Master money matters related to your job such as negotiating a raise, using your expense account, and surviving temporary unemployment.
- Plan for retirement.
- Cope with major financial transitions such as living together, marriage, and having children.

Achieving your financial goals isn't as difficult or as hopeless as you might think. All it takes is a long-term strategy, determination, and this book.

Everything
COLLEGE
DIDN'T
TEACH
YOU
ABOUT
MONEY

1

GETTING ORGANIZED

P AUL LOOKED UP AS SUE WALKED IN LOADED WITH
shopping bags. "I thought you were just going along to
help Carol shop."

"Paul, all I bought was a sweater and a pair of jeans. And the
sweater was on sale. What's the big deal?"

"I've been paying our bills and we have $30 left in our check-
ing account. We still have $150 in school-loan payments to make.
Neither of us is getting paid for ten days. How did you pay for
those new things?"

"With my credit card. Don't worry. We have a $2,000 credit
limit."

"Your credit card—that reminds me. Why did we have a $60
interest charge this month? I thought you paid that bill last
month."

"Oh, I thought you paid it. I guess it just slipped through the
cracks. Well, it's only $60. Don't worry about it. We make
$80,000 between us. We're rich."

"Sue, that's what you said when we bought the living room
furniture and the car. Rich people have more than $30 in their
checking accounts."

"Oh, you're just grouchy because you haven't eaten all day.
Come on, let's go out to dinner. Just give me a minute to change
into my new sweater."

Rachel returned from lunch with her friend Lisa and slumped
into her chair feeling depressed. Lisa had spent most of the hour

chatting about her upcoming vacation in London. London! Rachel barely could scrape together the funds to finance her share of a one-week stay in a beach house in Rehoboth Beach, Delaware.

During last summer's misery of cramming for the bar exam, Rachel and Lisa had fantasized about their new lives as lawyers —not impoverished law students. They figured their salaries, even as first-year associates, would mean designer clothes instead of shopping the racks at Loehmann's, real furniture to replace their family cast-offs, and European vacations.

What most upset Rachel was that she and Lisa earned roughly the same salary. "Are your parents helping you out with the trip?" Rachel had asked Lisa suspiciously. "Of course not," Lisa answered. "I've been saving $30 a week all year. Why don't you join me? The charter flights are a great deal."

Rachel was too embarrassed to reveal the meager sum in her savings account—$300—most of which was a birthday gift from her grandparents. She had meant to save, but she could barely make it from paycheck to paycheck. She felt a twinge of guilt remembering those Italian pumps she had paid $100 for last night (they were marked down from $160); Saturday's $40 facial (she worked hard and deserved a little pampering); and the $30 she had blown on dinner in that new French restaurant (who felt like cooking after eight hours of researching a legal brief?).

She'd never get to Europe at this rate, she thought, noticing the phone message on her desk. It was from Diane, her college roommate who lived in Boston. Diane invited her for a visit. "With those new excursion fares, it will only cost $150 round trip," Diane coaxed.

"Maybe Diane is right," Rachel thought. She did need a change of scenery. Anyway, they hadn't seen each other for ages. Rachel hung up, feeling more cheerful as she dialed her travel agent.

It was the Sunday evening before his tax return was due. Tom, surrounded by bills and receipts, was kneeling on the floor of his study and thumbing through the messy bottom drawer of his file cabinet.

Tom was sure that somewhere in the drawer were receipts from his doctor and bills for medicine that he had thrown in during the year. He was also trying to locate the sales slip for his new stereo system. He could document major deductions if he could only find those receipts. He looked at his watch. It was 10:20 P.M. and he wasn't close to finishing. This would take at least three or four hours and he had a busy day at the office tomorrow.

"Maybe I'll just guesstimate these items," Tom thought. The Internal Revenue Service would never know, unless he was audited. "So I'll spend a few nights lying awake, worrying about an audit. I guess that's worth the couple of hundred dollars I'll save by claiming these deductions," he thought. His stomach tightened. How he hated tax time. Last year he had resolved never to go through this agony again. Yet he never seemed to find the time to set up a more organized system.

Meanwhile, he had to get through tonight's mess. "Let's see, my root canal work was about $250, my eyeglasses were about $100," he estimated, jotting down the figures on a sheet of paper.

Sue and Paul, Rachel, and Tom are in the same predicament. They all need some type of financial system to keep their personal finances under control. The system should consist of four elements: controlling expenses, paying bills, establishing a savings program, and keeping records for tax and other purposes.

Sue and Paul earn plenty of money, but not enough to support their spending habits. They have been on a buying binge—new furniture, new clothes, new car, dinners out several nights a week, expensive vacations. Compounding their financial problems is their haphazard bill-paying system. Each assumes—often wrongly—that the other is keeping an eye on the bills. This chapter will describe how an organized bill-paying system can maximize savings and guarantee timely payments.

Rachel has no discipline to save, nor does she have a clear picture of her long-term financial goals. To develop sound financial habits that will enable her to do the things she wants—such as take a European vacation—she needs to keep track of her expenses, budget for necessities, and set up a savings plan. This chapter will show her—and you—how to do it.

As Tom is painfully learning, you can't simply pay your bills and forget about them. You must keep records showing how much you've spent and on what. Record-keeping allows you to substantiate tax deductions that could be worth hundreds or even thousands of dollars every year. Maintaining accurate records saves time and aggravation when you need to review past financial transactions. This chapter will teach you how to set up a filing system to include personal documents, income records, medical expenses, and other items.

DETERMINING YOUR NET WORTH

The first step in getting organized is filling out a personal balance sheet that lists your **assets** and **liabilities**. That statement indicating your **net worth** is a barometer of your financial health and the base from which you can make all future money decisions, such as setting saving and spending goals.

Filling out the form on pages 6–7 is a handy exercise that will tell you a great deal about your financial condition. It's also good practice. You will be asked to repeat this exercise every time you apply for a mortgage or other bank loan.

Tips on Figuring Your Net Worth
For assets:

Personal property: To determine the current value of your home, check with local real estate agents and the classified advertisements in local newspapers. Your home is worth what it would bring on the market minus sales costs.

Jewelry, art, and other collectibles: Ask appraisers and read classified ads in newspapers and magazines to place a value on your
items.

Stocks and bonds: Their value can be calculated by looking up
current prices in the newspaper.

Insurance and annuities: Ask your insurance company to supply
you with the figures for the cash and conversion values.

For liabilities:

"Current bills" refers to bills you have received but haven't
paid (not your annual expenditures). For loans, count only the
principal due on your car, education, and other loans, not the
interest. Your lender can tell you what it is if you don't know.

Determine your net worth once a year to measure whether
your net worth has grown and by how much.

CONTROLLING EXPENSES

Financial control consists of learning how you spend your
money and then changing those patterns to suit your goals. Your
goals should include saving for both near- and long-term plans
and having sufficient cash to cover unexpected expenditures. If,
like Sue, Paul, and Rachel, you need a clearer picture of where
your money goes, after figuring your net worth, set up a table
for charting your expenses, as shown on page 8.

To figure expenses, take your checkbook and credit card records (if you have them), and estimate how much you spend in
each of the categories in Table 1:1 . To determine the amount
you normally spend on food, entertainment, or other categories
where your records are sketchy, reconstruct a normal month
through your checking account records and by jotting down
what you spent in the most recent two-month period.

There may be some overlap of categories as shown in Alan's
sample worksheet (Table 1:2, page 9). Alan, a 29-year-old engi-

Date_____

Assets

Cash and Investments
    Checking accounts $_____
    Savings accounts   _____
    Money market funds   _____
    Outstanding loans to others _____
    Stocks _____
    Bonds _____
    Certificates of deposit _____
    Treasury bills _____
    Gold, silver (at today's value) _____
    Cash value of insurance and _____
      annuities
    Company profit-sharing plans _____
    Retirement accounts: IRAs and _____
      KEOGHs
    Real estate _____
    Other _____

Total Cash and Investments $_____

Personal Property

Car $_____
House _____
Furniture _____
Jewelry, antiques, art, furniture _____
Other _____

Total Personal Property $_____

Total Assets $_____

Liabilities

Current Bills

Mortgage or rent	$_____	
Charge account balances	_____	
Utilities	_____	
Taxes	_____	
Insurance premiums	_____	
Medical	_____	
Furniture	_____	
Other	_____	
Total Bills		$_____

Loans

Home mortgage	$_____	
Education	_____	
Car	_____	
Loans against life insurance	_____	
Other	_____	
Total Loans		$_____
Total Liabilities		$_____

Total Assets Minus Total Liabilities Equals Net Worth

$_____

Table 1:1—Expense Comparison

Category	Amount spent 1st half of year	Amount spent last half of year	Total	% of take-home pay
Fixed Expenses				
Rent or Mortgage				
Food				
Utilities				
Transportation and Car Repair				
Insurance Premiums				
Medical Bills				
Loan Payments: car, education, other				
Flexible Expenses				
Clothing				
Personal Care				
Vacations, Hobbies, and Entertainment				
Dues and Subscriptions				
Gifts				
Charitable Contributions				
Savings and Investments				
Total				

neer with a $37,000 gross income, puts his expenses for dining out under "vacations, hobbies, and entertainment" rather than under "food" because he considers dinners out with friends and dates as social expenses. For this reason, his food budget falls on the low side and his entertainment expenses are on the high side. Alan's transportation costs are low because he drives to work in a car that was a gift from his parents. He lives in a rented apartment and has paid back his school loans. He makes no monthly loan or mortgage payments. These factors enable him to save a hefty 31 percent of his take-home pay, or 20 percent of his gross pay, placing him in an enviable financial situation.

When you fill in the worksheet (Table 1:1), it will serve as a snapshot of your budget. It reflects personal choices you have made. For instance, your housing costs may be on the high side

Table 1:2—Sample Expense Comparison with $37,000 Income

Gross Pay: $37,000
minus Federal Tax: $9,827
minus FICA
(Social Security) Tax: $2,479
minus State Tax: $1,543
Take-home pay: $23,151

Category	Amount spent 1st half of year	Amount spent last half of year	Total	% of take-home pay
Fixed Expenses				
Rent or Mortgage	$2,000	$2,600	$4,600	20%
Food	450	480	930	4
Utilities	456	490	946	4
Transportation and Car Repair	1,150	550	1,700	7
Insurance Premiums	300	270	570	3
Medical Bills	220	220	440	2
Loan Payments: car, education, other	0	0	0	0
Flexible Expenses				
Clothing	600	1,360	1,960	8%
Personal Care	400	400	800	3
Vacations, Hobbies, and Entertainment	1,530	1,470	3,000	13
Dues and Subscriptions	135	230	365	2
Gifts	150	200	350	2
Charitable Contributions	50	150	200	1
Savings and Investments	1,500	5,790	7,290	31
Total	8,941	14,210	23,151	100

and your transportation costs minimal because you've chosen to spend more on rent to live close to your office in an urban area. By living in the city rather than in a suburb, you can walk or take a bus or subway to work, eliminating the cost of car ownership. Geography plays a part in your budget, too; housing and entertainment costs will be higher if you live in New York City than in Tulsa.

Filling in the numbers and computing the percentage of your income spent on various items should help you see where your money goes, a necessary step for setting reasonable spending and saving goals.

Because we all have our own money quirks, setting goals is a highly individualized process. But these general guidelines should be helpful:

- Savings and investments should be budgeted as carefully as housing and food expenses. If you are a passive saver and expect excess funds to dribble into this category, you'll never save enough. Set as your savings goal at least 10 percent of your gross income.

- If meeting that 10 percent savings goal looks like a long stretch, take a hard look at the flexible expense categories. Do any of the "clothing," "personal care," or "vacations, hobbies, and entertainment" categories exceed 15 percent of your take-home pay? If so, it's a good place to start trimming. It's much easier to cut back on clothes, facials, haircuts, and vacations than on rent or grocery bills.

- There is no right or wrong way to divide your income pie, as long as you're not spending more than your salary or failing to meet savings and investment goals. Guidelines set by experts won't always fit your situation. For example, financial experts caution against spending more than one-fourth of your take-home pay on rent, but try renting a New York City apartment or buying a San Francisco condominium by sticking to this advice. If you spend more than 30 percent of your take-home pay on housing, that's okay, but you'll have to cut back in other places. If you're just starting out and are saddled with debts for your education, your car, your furniture, and your working wardrobe, meeting that 10 percent savings goal this year may be impossible. Your first priority must be to pay off those debts, especially if they are carrying 20 percent or higher interest charges.

Use the worksheet as a tool to help rearrange your expenses.

Table 1:3—Expense Comparison for Sue and Paul

ss Pay: $80,000
ıs Federal Tax: $23,568 (assumes they file a joint return)
ıs FICA
ial Security) Tax: $5,065
ıs State Tax: $3,000
e-home pay: $48,367

Category	Amount spent 1st half of year	Amount spent last half of year	Total	% of take-home pay
ed Expenses				
t or Mortgage	$4,800	$5,100	$9,900	20%
d	1,320	1,700	3,020	6
ities	900	750	1,650	3
ısportation and Car epair	1,500	1,320	2,820	6
ırance Premiums	1,440	1,500	2,940	6
dical Bills	600	600	1,200	2
n Payments: car, ducation, other	3,900	3,900	7,800	16
xible Expenses				
thing	2,400	2,460	4,860	10%
sonal Care	1,200	1,000	2,200	5
ations, Hobbies, nd Entertainment	4,050	4,200	8,250	17
es and Subscriptions	300	340	640	1
ts	500	500	1,000	2
ıritable Contributions	250	300	550	1
ings and nvestments	700	837	1,537	3
al	23,860	24,507	48,367	98

te: Because of rounding, figures do not add up to 100%.

For example, after doing a sample budget (Table 1:3 above), Paul and Sue decided to readjust their spending habits to save $7,000 this year—almost 10 percent of their gross pay. It's an ambitious goal, given their spending patterns. To accomplish it, they concentrated on these areas:

- Vacations. They took a three-week vacation to Europe last year that cost $4,000. By setting a $2,000 limit on their upcoming vacation, they felt they would be able to channel an extra $2,000 of their earnings into savings this year.
- Entertainment. Instead of meeting friends for dinner and the theater on the weekends, they suggested the movies and dessert.
- Minor indulgences. Sue cut her monthly manicure and facial to every other month. Dinners out were restricted to twice a week.
- Hobbies. Paul stopped buying expensive gadgets for his camera every few weeks.
- Clothing. They limited their clothing purchases to $100 a month for both of them.

You may discover a problem using the worksheet: You can't figure out how much you've spent in each expense category because your checkbook transactions and credit card bills don't reflect all your spending patterns. For instance, your checkbook shows that you've cashed a $50 check every few days, but you don't know what you've spent it on.

A simple solution is to jot down what you spend in a daily expense calendar or budget book. It will remind you of the cab fares, lunch tabs, and other incidental purchases you made and forgot. Even if the idea of a daily expense calendar sounds like too much trouble, try it for two or three months. Doing the exercise for a short time will give you a better idea of the items you buy that prevent you from building up your savings.

To track your progress, fill out this worksheet every month or so until you're satisfied with how your money is allocated.

ESTABLISHING A SAVINGS PROGRAM

For young professionals, establishing a savings program is as important in your overall financial system as controlling expenditures. Why bother to save at all when you are starting out? One reason is that it's not going to get easier to save when you earn more, especially if you've fallen into the trap of not exerting control over your finances. Overspending leads to a dangerous cycle: Need forces you to borrow money at high interest rates, pushing you deeper and deeper into debt.

Mastering a savings system is easier when you have less money and fewer family responsibilities. Setting aside a fixed amount each month is the best way to develop sound financial discipline.

How much to save depends on your situation. As we said earlier, a worthy goal is at least 10 percent of your gross pay. For instance, say you earn $30,000 per year and take home $20,000. Savings of $3,000 to $4,500 per year is good. If hefty education debts make that goal unattainable, however, aim for 5 to 8 percent of your gross salary. The amount you set aside is not as important as learning to save a fixed amount on a regular basis, at least in the beginning years of financial independence.

How much savings is enough? You don't have to worry about having too much money saved—there's no such thing. You need at least enough savings to build a comfortable cushion in case of an emergency—the loss of your job, major car repairs, unforeseen dental or medical expenses. The cushion is important because if you don't have the equivalent of three months to six months of living expenses saved, you may be forced to borrow money at high interest rates when an emergency occurs.

If you deposit your paycheck in a checking account and then pay your bills and promptly spend what's left over, you will find saving any amount nearly impossible. Therefore, financial planners recommend a system called "Paying yourself first." As soon as you receive your paycheck, write a check to yourself for 5 to 15 percent of it. Deposit it in your savings account. Or you can deposit your entire paycheck in an interest-bearing money market or bank account, use that account for savings, and write yourself a separate check to cover your monthly expenses. Place that check in your checking account, and once you spend it, don't withdraw any more until your next paycheck arrives.

If you know your financial discipline is weak, a painless way to save is to join a company savings plan. Find out if your company offers one—it's a common fringe benefit. A company savings plan operates on the principle that you won't miss what you never had in your pocket. The company automatically deducts 1 to 6 percent of your paycheck and invests it for you in stocks and other securities. You can withdraw all or a portion of the savings when you need it, although the company will have restrictions on how often you may make withdrawals. An extra incentive to join is that many employers will match at least part of your contribution to the plan; for instance, the company may add 50 cents to every dollar you contribute. Some companies even match your contribution dollar for dollar. Generally, you have to work for the company for a certain amount of time—three to five years is typical—to receive the company's contributions when you withdraw money from the plan.

PAYING BILLS

Establishing a bill-paying schedule is the next step in your personal financial system. The best method is to set aside one convenient time each month and pay all the bills that have accumulated.

You may want to schedule your bill-paying system to maximize your float. Float is the time it takes a check you've written to clear your bank and be deducted from your account. When your money is in an interest-bearing checking account—and it should be—it earns interest until the time the check clears. Here are three easy ways to squeeze the most float out of your dollars:

1. Pay your bills just before their due date, not the minute you receive them or beyond the due date. (Chronic lateness in bill-paying will mar your credit record.)

2. When given the choice of paying by check or credit card, use the credit card. The monthly billing cycle means your money will stay in your checking account longer. Note: If you won't have the money in your checking account to cover the purchase when the bill arrives, pay for it now or don't buy it.

3. Pay late in the week or just before holidays.

If you have trouble finding time to pay your bills, ask if your bank offers "pay by phone" services. Instead of sitting down with your bills, checkbook, stamps, and envelopes, the service allows you to pay bills simply by dialing the phone. Typically, you call your bank, tell the operator your telephone account number and personal identification code, the amount of the check, to whom it goes, and the date you want it paid. The bank will do the rest through electronic data transmissions. Instead of receiving canceled checks each month, the bank will send you a record of your transactions.

Typical fees for this service are a flat $2 to $3 per month and/or 15 cents per transaction. Many banks offer the service free. In addition, you may be required to keep a minimum balance in your checking account. Most pay-by-phone systems operate twenty-four hours a day, allowing you to pay bills at your leisure. When you know you will be out of town, you can instruct the bank in advance to pay your bills on time.

KEEPING RECORDS

Of course, once you pay your bills you must keep your receipts. But that's only a small part of the paper you need to store to keep your financial affairs in order. An organized filing system will help you avoid the pitfalls facing Tom at tax time and the rest of the year. Consulting your financial records will be necessary to look up the price you paid for an investment, to check the coverage offered on an insurance policy, or to read the fine print on an old loan agreement.

Take a stack of manila folders and arrange them in a desk or file drawer, one folder per each of the following categories that pertain to you:

- Income records. Keep W-2 forms from employers, alimony records if you have them, and income statements from interest and dividends (1099 forms). Keep pay stubs if medical coverage or parking fees are deducted from your paycheck. Your yearly summary statement may list only the taxes and FICA (Social Security taxes) taken out, not the other deductions. If you're an independent consultant, a free-lancer, or a commissioned salesperson you must keep records of all money received during the year.

  If you receive income from other sources such as rental property or gifts of money, keep those records, too. You can use your checkbook, with its deposit statements, as your cash-receipts record.
- Personal papers. Include birth certificates, divorce or separation decrees, marriage licenses, and passports.
- Canceled checks. After you reconcile your monthly bank statements, file the checks chronologically. In case of a tax audit, the checks will document donations and other expenses. You may want to include monthly bank statements, deposit slips, and a list of all bank accounts by name and number. If you pay your bills through a cash management account (Merrill Lynch CMA, for instance) you won't receive canceled checks, only a statement with the names of the accounts paid. You must keep those statements as your record.
- Life, health, and disability insurance. Keep the policies, records of claims, receipts for premium payments, names of beneficiaries, and the names and addresses of your insurance companies and your agents.
- Medical expenses. To claim tax deductions you must document costs for items such as doctor, hospital, and medicine

bills, eyeglasses, laboratory tests, braces, contraceptives, and transportation to and from medical services.

- Car. Keep all papers relating to your car's care and ownership: title, bill of sale, loan records, insurance policy, auto club membership, repair bills, maintenance records, and warranty.
- Housing expenses. Keep documents relating to the purchase or lease of your home, including deeds, mortgage papers, title papers, title and homeowner's insurance policies, and receipts for major purchases and repairs. When you sell your home, the cost for permanent capital improvements such as new carpeting or the addition of a sun deck can be added to the cost of the property, reducing your tax liability.
- Investments. You may want to keep a separate file for each of your investments: stocks, bonds, mutual funds, money market mutual funds, bank accounts, and Individual Retirement Accounts or KEOGH plans. To compute your capital gains tax, make future investment decisions, and keep track of your overall financial plan, you should keep the following for each investment: the date you bought it, the purchase price, dividend and interest payments, date of sale, sale price, and profit or loss from the sale. You should keep records of stock and bond transactions for three years after you dispose of them. In case you are audited you would need to show the original price you paid for the securities. *Note:* The Internal Revenue Service can audit any return filed within the last three years.
- Tax returns. Keep federal, state, and city tax returns (as well as the worksheets, receipts, and evidence of expenses and income) for at least three years from the date due, and keep documents supporting any major or unusual tax deductions for seven years. Keep your returns for three years if you plan to income average. There is no statute of limitations on tax returns in cases where the IRS suspects fraud.
- Sales slips, receipts, and warranties. Keep receipts of major purchases such as furniture or appliances so you can calculate

if what you spent exceeds the standard deduction for sales tax on your federal tax return. Keep all guarantees, warranties, and dates and costs of repairs.

- Loan records. Keep records of payments you make, plus loans you make to others. If your bank doesn't send you a statement of interest paid during the year, add it up yourself.
- Credit card bills. File all credit card bills so you can track expenditures for budgeting, identify tax deductible items, and determine interest deductions.
- Business expenses. Your company probably reimburses you for most items, but keep track of your unreimbursed costs. You can deduct from your taxes all unreimbursed dues to professional organizations, job-hunting expenses, business telephone calls, job and investment-related magazine subscriptions, and travel costs to visit clients. The IRS currently requires a written diary of travel and entertainment expenses. To deduct depreciation and investment tax credits for a home computer, you must keep a diary of time spent using it for business. If you have a free-lance or part-time job, or are attending a professional convention at your own expense, keep a diary of nonreimbursible expenses. The diary should list hotel bills, transportation costs, meals, and telephone calls. Save receipts.
- Contributions to charities, church, and other organizations.
- Miscellaneous deductions. Keep records of income tax return preparation fees and job-related education expenses so you can deduct them. Also keep track of any adjustments to income such as moving expenses or casualty losses.

Each year after you file your tax return, start a new set of folders and store the previous year's records. Files that aren't directly related to your income taxes, for example, receipts and warranties or car ownership records, can be kept indefinitely. Records of installment payments such as car or educational loans should be kept until you pay off the item.

Note: Keep originals of important documents such as birth certificates, citizenship papers, marriage license, adoption papers, divorce papers, wills, car titles, contracts, and household inventory in a safe-deposit box.

Sue and Paul have worked out a better bill-paying system. Once a month they go through their accumulated bills, reconcile their joint checking account, discuss what they've spent, and pay each bill.

Money is still a sticky issue, but they haven't argued about it for three weeks, a new record. After four months on a spending diet they have accumulated $1,500 in savings. They are still a bit far from their $7,000 goal, but they are encouraged by their progress.

"You know, I hardly miss all the dinners out," Paul said. "And I'm becoming a much better cook."

"I've noticed," Sue replied. "If I wasn't walking so much [she was trying to save on taxi fares] I'd probably be fatter."

Rachel confided her financial problems to Barbara, a friend at work. "You should join the company savings plan. It helped me," Barbara suggested.

Under the plan, 6 percent of Rachel's salary was automatically deducted from her paycheck and set aside in an account. The law firm matched her contribution 50 cents to each dollar she saved. She wouldn't receive the law firm's contribution until she had worked there four years. However, she could withdraw her own money any time. But she didn't. Rachel regarded that money as her long-term savings—not to be touched except for an emergency. To save for short-term goals, such as a trip to Europe next summer and a condominium, she put aside an extra $50 a month in her savings account.

Sure, Rachel had temporary lapses. But instead of buying expensive clothes on impulse, she browsed for sales and rewarded herself with makeup or a new paperback book. She found that having focused goals, such as a two-week trip to Europe, made it easier to pass up items she didn't really need.

Tom finished paying some bills and added the receipts to a messy stack of papers accumulating on his desk. He envisioned the stack growing higher and higher. No, he wasn't going to let it happen again!

Where were those manila folders he had bought two months ago? He pulled them out and started labeling: credit cards, bank accounts, medical, car, etc. Next, he took the stack of bills and receipts and divided them into piles.

Two hours later Tom's desk was clean. In his desk drawer was an organized filing system. Each month, after paying the bills, he would sort them and place them in the appropriate file. Now that he was organized, tax time would no longer be an ordeal.

2

TAXES

I T IS MID-MARCH AND THE THOUGHT OF FILING THIS
year's income tax returns is afflicting everyone with dread.

Tom dialed Joan's number, hoping she would be home.

She answered on the fifth ring. "Sorry it took so long. I was
standing on a chair searching the top shelf of my closet, looking
for some receipts. I'm in the middle of doing my taxes," she
explained.

Tom invited her to the movies.

"I'd love to go. But if I stopped now, I'd never finish. Thanks
for asking."

"Joan, there's no need to struggle. You can use the EZ form
with eleven lines," Tom said. "That's what I'm going to do."

"That's a dumb idea. You shouldn't use that form. It's really
intended for students. You may save time, but you'll lose deductions you're entitled to take."

Tom was sorry he had called. If what she said was true—and
it probably was (she was a lawyer, after all)—he would have to
forget his plans for a speedy tax-filing session.

"Well, I'll have to check into it more thoroughly. But I'm not
going to let it spoil the rest of my day. Are you sure you don't
want to come to the movies?"

"Okay, you talked me into it. Why don't you pick me up in
twenty minutes?"

Rachel and her friend Barbara were discussing a silk blouse they had just admired in a shop window. "I can't afford it now. But I'll be getting my tax refund in a month or so," Barbara said.

"How did you manage to get a refund? You're making more money than I am," Rachel asked.

"It's simple. I income average. You can probably do it, too, since this is your first year out of law school," Barbara replied. "I saved $1,100 the first year, $900 last year, and $500 this year."

"It seems like a big hassle," Rachel answered. "I don't have copies of my past returns. Anyway, my parents helped me during law school. I'm not sure I can prove I was self-supporting."

"Rachel, you can always get back copies of your tax returns by writing to the IRS. And you may save yourself hundreds of dollars. How can you be so lazy?"

Rachel had to admit Barbara had a point.

Sue removed the mail from the box, spotting the envelope from the Internal Revenue Service. She ripped it open as she walked upstairs.

The computerized letter said that the IRS wanted more information about business expenses claimed on last year's tax return.

"Bad news, Paul. We're getting audited."

Paul studied the letter. "It doesn't give us many clues. At least we kept good records. I guess there's nothing to worry about. So why am I so worried?" he asked, pacing around the living room.

"Let's call Uncle Jerry for advice. He's the best accountant we know," Sue replied, picking up the phone.

Tax planning is no longer the reserve of the rich. Inflation has pushed even the beginning salaries of young professionals into high marginal tax brackets, making planning a crucial money-saving tool. Whether you earn $20,000 as a single or $100,000 as a couple filing jointly, you can save thousands of dollars each year by taking advantage of tax credits and deductions.

There is nothing illegal or immoral about this. As Appeals

Court Judge Learned Hand said in a 1934 decision: "Anyone may arrange his affairs that his taxes shall be as low as possible; he is not bound to choose that which will best pay the Treasury; there is not even a patriotic duty to increase one's taxes."

DETERMINING YOUR MARGINAL TAX BRACKET

Your first step in tax planning is to figure your **marginal tax bracket,** which determines the impact of any tax deductions you claim. As Table 2:1 on page 25 illustrates, the more you earn, the more tax you pay on the last dollar earned.

There is a common misconception about figuring your marginal tax bracket. Many people believe that you pay the top tax rate on all your income. That's not true. The marginal tax bracket refers to the percentage the government takes of every dollar above a certain income level.

For example, as the chart on page 25 indicates, if you are single and earn $45,000, you're in a 42 percent federal tax bracket. That does not mean you pay 42 percent of your income, or $18,900, to Uncle Sam. It means you pay a base tax of $10,319 plus 42 percent of the amount earned over $41,500 ($1,470). Your federal tax liability would be $11,789 or 26 percent of your total income, not 42 percent.

But to get a true picture of your total marginal tax bracket, you must include in your calculations additional state and local income taxes. So, if in the above example you paid 5 percent* of your income in state and local taxes, your total marginal tax bracket is 47 percent (42 percent federal plus 5 percent state and local).

*This is net of federal income tax savings, since state and local taxes are deductible on your federal tax return. For example, if you paid 9% in state and local taxes, or $4,050, and you were in the 42% federal marginal tax bracket, you would save $1,701 (42% of $4,050) on your federal tax. Thus, your net state tax would be $2,349 ($4,050 minus $1,701) or 5% of your income.

Here's how a married couple filing a joint return would figure their marginal tax bracket, assuming their total income is $55,000 and they pay 4 percent in state and local taxes (net of federal tax savings):

1. Their base tax is $9,772, plus 38 percent of the amount they earn over $45,800. That means their federal marginal tax bracket is 38 percent.
2. Their total marginal tax bracket, including state and local taxes, is 42 percent (38 percent federal plus 4 percent state and local).

Use this tax rate schedule to determine your marginal tax bracket.

FILING YOUR 1040 FORM

The complexity of your tax situation determines which form you file: the 1040 EZ, the 1040A "short" form, or the 1040 "long" form. Don't be so eager to get your taxes done that you use a shorter form than necessary and overpay. Whatever the shorter forms save you in time they could cost you in money. These details will help you select the best one.

The 1040 EZ

What could be easier than a tax form with only eleven lines? Therein lies its appeal. To file it, you must be single, have no dependents, and have a taxable income of $50,000 or less. You can't use this form if you earned more than $400 in interest and dividend income during the year from stocks or money market funds or if you contributed to an Individual Retirement Account. Because you could overlook deductions you are entitled to take by using the EZ form, pass it up unless all your income comes from a small salary or you're a student with income from part-time jobs.

Table 2:1—1984 Tax Rate Schedules for Estimating Your Marginal Tax Bracket

If taxable income is over—	But not over—	The tax is:	Of the amount over—
Single Taxpayers			
$0	$2,300	0	
2,300	3,400	0 + 11%	$2,300
3,400	4,400	$121 + 12%	3,400
4,400	6,500	241 + 14%	4,400
6,500	8,500	535 + 15%	6,500
8,500	10,800	835 + 16%	8,500
10,800	12,900	1,203 + 18%	10,800
12,900	15,000	1,581 + 20%	12,900
15,000	18,200	2,001 + 23%	15,000
18,200	23,500	2,737 + 26%	18,200
23,500	28,800	4,115 + 30%	23,500
28,800	34,100	5,705 + 34%	28,800
34,100	41,500	7,507 + 38%	34,100
41,500	55,300	10,319 + 42%	41,500
55,300	81,800	16,115 + 48%	55,300
81,800	—	28,835 + 50%	81,800
Married Filing Joint Returns			
$0	$3,400	0	
3,400	5,500	0 + 11%	$3,400
5,500	7,600	$231 + 12%	5,500
7,600	11,900	483 + 14%	7,600
11,900	16,000	1,085 + 16%	11,900
16,000	20,200	1,741 + 18%	16,000
20,200	24,600	2,497 + 22%	20,200
24,600	29,900	3,465 + 25%	24,600
29,900	35,200	4,790 + 28%	29,900
35,200	45,800	6,274 + 33%	35,200
45,800	60,000	9,772 + 38%	45,800
60,000	85,600	15,168 + 42%	60,000
85,600	109,400	25,920 + 45%	85,600
109,400	162,400	36,630 + 49%	109,400
162,400	—	62,600 + 50%	162,400

(Source: Internal Revenue Service.)

The 1040 Short vs. Long Forms

Many people automatically file the 1040A short form because they think they don't have enough itemized deductions to use the long form. (Anyone earning over $50,000 must file the long form.) To encourage taxpayers to use the shorter form, the Internal Revenue Service expanded the 1040A by including lines for IRA contributions and child-care credits. But using the short form may be a costly mistake.

That long, miserable form may save you enough to take an extra vacation this year. With the long form you can itemize deductions. It's to your benefit to itemize whenever you have large deductions for expenses that, when totaled, exceed the **zero bracket amount** (tax jargon for the old standard deduction, which is the built-in deduction the government gives to non-itemizers to offset income). The zero bracket amount is $3,400 for a married couple filing jointly, $2,300 for singles, and $1,700 for married people filing separate returns. You won't find the zero bracket amount written anywhere on your tax return; it's already built into the tax tables. Inflation has eroded the value of the zero bracket amount, which hasn't changed since 1978, so it may pay to itemize this year even if you never did before.

Unless you think your deductions will exceed the zero bracket amount substantially, however, don't itemize. You could spend several hours adding up your deductions only to find that you have $2,310 in deductions, which will save you exactly $4 in taxes if you are in a 40 percent tax bracket.

Even if your deductions don't exceed the zero bracket amount, you may want to file the long form to take advantage of little-known deductions such as job-related moving expenses, or to compute your taxes using income averaging. Those items are called "adjustments to income"—they are really deductions in disguise—and you can get them without itemizing as long as you file the long form. In other cases—if you want to file for a time extension on your return, use a residential energy tax credit for buying insulation, or if you paid a penalty for cashing in a certificate of deposit prematurely—then you must use the long form.

Tom zipped through the EZ form in fifteen minutes. It was so easy that he was tempted to stop there. But he realized that Joan was probably right. To be sure, he filled out the EZ and the long form and compared the difference in the size of his refund.

Filing his taxes certainly was less of a chore than it had been in the past, thanks to his record-keeping system. Laying all his files on the dining room table, he began working, deducting his Individual Retirement Account contribution, charitable donations, and subscriptions to trade publications. There weren't enough medical expenses to claim a deduction this year. It took three hours, but his refund grew by $200, making the time spent well worth it.

He was self-confident enough to admit when he was wrong. The least he could do was take Joan to a good restaurant next weekend.

Should Couples File Joint or Separate Returns?

Most married couples should file a joint return. But there are a few exceptions where filing separately could reduce taxes. For example, only medical expenses that exceed 5 percent of adjusted gross income can be deducted. If one spouse earns substantially less than the other and incurs large medical expenses, filing separately could allow the lower-earning spouse to deduct those expenses. A couple with a joint adjusted gross income of $40,000 and medical expenses of $1,500 can't deduct them, but one spouse with an adjusted gross income of $14,000 could deduct $800, if the expenses were his or hers alone.

The biggest disadvantage to filing separately is that marginal tax rates are much higher than they are for joint returns. For instance, a couple earning $60,000 ($40,000 and $20,000) will owe $15,168 in federal taxes if they file jointly versus $15,713 if they file separately, a $545 difference. If you're not sure which method to use, figure your taxes both ways and compare.

If you and your spouse have different last names you can still file a joint return. You must separate your names with an "and"; for example, David Smith "and" Mary Marks. Also, make sure the first name matches the first Social Security number. Try to be consistent each year, because if you switch the order of names or Social Security numbers you may confuse the IRS computer and delay the processing of your return. Include a copy of your marriage license with your tax returns so there's no question you're married.

The Marriage Penalty

No one ever said life is fair. Thanks to a quirk in the tax law called the "marriage penalty," two-income married couples owe more in taxes than two singles who live together and earn the same total income. There's some relief for married couples, however: They can deduct 10 percent of the first $30,000 of the earned income of the spouse who earns less.

Take a married couple such as Sue and Paul. She earns $35,000, he earns $45,000. The "marriage adjustment deduction" entitles them to take a $3,000 deduction from Sue's salary, lowering their taxable income from $80,000 to $77,000, and resulting in a tax savings of $1,260.

The higher the tax bracket, the greater the savings. For example, for a couple in a 30 percent marginal tax bracket, a $3,000 deduction would lower their tax bill by $900, while a couple in a 50 percent marginal bracket would save $1,500. Only couples where both spouses earn $30,000 or more can take the full $3,000 deduction.

How to File for an Extension

If you are unable to complete your tax return by April 15, don't worry. You can get an extension. You don't even need a good excuse. To receive an automatic four-month extension—no questions asked by the IRS—simply file Form 4868. Extensions are granted to those who file a long form as well as a 1040A.

The procedure is easy. Just mail Form 4868 to your local IRS Service Center along with a check for the estimated tax you owe by midnight April 15. (See Appendix III for complete listing of addresses of service centers.) You must include the check because the extension is for filing your return, not for paying your tax bill. Of course, if you are going to receive a refund, no estimated taxes are due.

When you do get around to filing your return, attach a duplicate of Form 4868 and pay any balance due or claim your refund. Should you need another extension beyond August 15, send in Form 2688 or write a letter to the IRS explaining why you need more time.

Taxpayers who are outside of the U.S. on April 15 receive an automatic extension until June 15. Should this apply to you, attach a note to your tax return when you do file, explaining that you were out of the country. Otherwise, you may be mistakenly charged penalties for late filing, a headache you don't need.

Penalties

The IRS imposes stiff penalties on procrastinators who owe them money. Anytime you owe the IRS money after April 15 you will be charged an interest rate based on the prevailing prime rate. The rate changes every six months, but from January 1 to June 30, 1985, it is 13 percent.

If you file Form 4868 but fail to pay your taxes, or underpay by more than 10 percent of the total tax due, you will be charged a penalty of one-half percent a month on the amount owed, in addition to the interest charge.

If you underpay the balance owed by 20 percent or more of the total tax due, you will be charged:

- A late penalty of one-half percent a month on the full amount owed.

- Plus an estimated tax penalty on part of the balance due, equal to the prevailing IRS interest rate (the 13 percent figure above), compounded daily from the time the estimated tax is due until April 15.

If you don't file Form 4868 at all, you will be charged an additional late filing penalty of 5 percent per month or fraction of a month on the amount owed. However, the combined late filing and late payment penalties levied cannot exceed 5 percent a month, and after the first five months it reverts to one-half percent per month until the balance is fully paid.

AVOIDING OVERPAYMENT ON YOUR TAXES

There's no reason to allow the government to hang on to more of your tax dollars than it is entitled—yet most of us do. If you expect a hefty tax refund this year, you probably have too much money withheld from your paycheck. Instead of allowing the government to hold on to your money interest-free, wouldn't you prefer to have the extra money working for you in a savings account? After all, it is yours. Of course, some people intentionally overwithhold as a method of forced savings.

However, if forced savings isn't your intention, you can keep more by having your employer adjust the amount of your pay kept each week and sent to the government to cover your income tax. The government figures if it doesn't do this, you may come up short on April 15. Reducing your withholding doesn't cut your tax bill. It simply keeps you from overpaying taxes during the year. Rather than get a refund every spring you get a fatter paycheck all year.

To adjust your withholding to match your tax bill, file a new W-4 (employee's withholding allowance) form with your employer immediately.

To fill out the W-4 form, you must first estimate the total amount of your itemized deductions such as medical expenses, interest payments, charitable contributions, and so forth. The easiest way to do this is to look at last year's total itemized deductions and then add any deductions you expect this year. Include estimates of deductions that are not itemized, such as IRAs or other retirement plans, alimony, moving expenses, business expenses, the "marriage" deduction, and business and other losses. Finally, you will need to include the estimated tax reduction due to income averaging and various tax credits (such as child-care expenses and political contributions). Now, fill out the W-4 according to the instructions on the form.

Each allowance acts as if it reduces your pay by about $1,000 and consequently reduces the federal income tax withheld. Be careful: If you take too many allowances, and withhold less than 80 percent of your total tax liability during the year, the IRS will charge you a penalty. If you claim more than fourteen exemptions on a W-4 form, your employer must send the form to the IRS.

How to Save Tax Money

Even if you're not overwithholding, you may be overpaying your taxes. The tax laws are so complex that even accountants have trouble keeping track of all the changes. Don't worry. You don't have to substitute the U.S. Tax Code for your bedtime reading. However, be aware of common techniques, deductions, and credits that could reduce your tax liability.

First, the difference between a **tax credit** and a **tax deduction**: Credits offset taxes you owe on a dollar-for-dollar basis while a deduction allows you to subtract that amount from your taxable income. For example, a $100 tax credit will reduce your tax bill by $100 regardless of your tax bracket. But in a 30 percent marginal tax bracket, you need $333 in deductions to trim $100 off your tax bill. Thus, credits are worth more to you than deductions.

Income Averaging

This is an alternate method for computing your taxes that has been especially valuable to young professionals. In 1984 Congress changed the rules on **income averaging**, thus greatly reducing the tax break. The new rules specify that to qualify, your current year's income must be 40 percent greater than the average of your income during the past three years. The old rules specified that your current year's income must be 20 percent greater than the average of the past four years.

You can use income averaging, however, if, like Rachel, your income has increased by several thousand dollars this year because you are earning a salary after years of attending school and working part-time. Or maybe you earned a fat raise this year. In either case, income averaging could reduce your tax bill because it allows you to figure your current year's tax by spreading your income over a four-year period.

To income average you need copies of your tax returns for the past three years and a Schedule G form. Don't give up if, for whatever reasons, you don't have copies of your past returns handy. You can get copies by filing Internal Revenue Service Form 4506, "Request for Copy of Tax Form," for each missing year. The cost is $5 for each year's return. You need only the pages that show your adjusted gross income and taxable income.

To qualify for income averaging you have to have been a U.S. resident or citizen for the last four years and in most cases must have provided at least 50 percent of your support during those years. If your parents claimed you as a dependent in any of those years, you probably aren't eligible. There are exceptions; for example, students who have worked prior to finishing all schooling. You can check the details by sending for a free copy of IRS publication 506, "Income Averaging." (See Appendix III for addresses.)

You also must pass a test of how much your earnings have grown. Here's how to test whether you can income average if you are single; your taxable income (after deductions) for each of the last three years was $10,000, $15,000, and $25,000; and this year you earned $45,000.

General rules	**Example**
1. Add your income in years one through three.	1. 10,000 + 15,000 + 25,000 = 50,000.
2. Average the total of years one through three. That figure is your average base period.	2. 50,000 ÷ 3 = 16,667
3. Take 40 percent* of your average base period and add it to your average base period.	3. 40% of 16,667 = 6,667 6,667 + 16,667 = 23,334
4. Subtract that total figure from this year's taxable income.	4. 40,000 − 23,334 = 16,666
5. If that figure exceeds $3,000* you qualify for income average; if it's under $3,000 you don't.	5. Yes.

*The 40 percent and $3,000 are written into the IRS rules and never vary.

For newly married couples who were single in the base-period years, the taxable income for those years is the sum of both partners' incomes.

There's a simple solution if you discover that income averaging could have saved you money in past years. File Form 1040X to amend your tax return. You can amend a tax return for up to three years from the date it was due. You should attach a Schedule G form to each of the 1040X forms you send. The IRS will send you a refund for the extra taxes you paid, plus interest.

Rachel studied the copies of her tax returns for the past three years. It looked like she would qualify for income averaging, but she had to work out the numbers. In year one, between college and law school, she worked full-time as a paralegal and her taxable income was $14,000. In years two and three, she had part-time and summer legal jobs, and her taxable income was $8,000 a year. Her annual salary this year was $25,000, but she hadn't worked the entire year, which brought her taxable income down to $18,500.

Here's how Rachel would test whether she qualified for income averaging (using the general rules on the previous chart):

1. 14,000 + 8,000 + 8,000 = 30,000.
2. 30,000 ÷ 3 = 10,000.
3. 40% of 10,000 = 4,000
   4,000 + 10,000 = 14,000
4. 18,500 − 14,000 = 4,500
5. 4,500 exceeds 3,000, so she qualifies.

There was more than a $400 difference in the amount of taxes she owed before and after income averaging. That $400 translated into the difference between Rachel owing about $100 in additional taxes or receiving a $250 refund. It wasn't as much as she had hoped, but it was still a windfall. She decided to save half and spend half.

Charitable Contributions

If you itemize you can deduct all your charitable contributions. The charity must be approved by the IRS, but all the major ones are. You can't deduct your professional services as a donation.

You may deduct travel expenses for attending charity functions. When you drive your own car, there is a flat mileage allowance of 12 cents a mile (as of January 1985) and you may deduct parking fees and bridge and highway tolls. Volunteers who use a taxi, bus, or train to get back and forth may deduct these expenses, but keep records that include how far you went and for what purpose.

You can gain a deduction by cleaning out your closets and donating old clothes, books, and furniture to a thrift shop affiliated with any recognized charity. The thrift shop will appraise the items and give you a receipt for the replacement value or ask you to specify the value yourself. Be realistic in your estimate, and don't value the goods based on any sentiment you may have for your old things. The IRS isn't sentimental when it evaluates your tax return. Beware: You can't donate your property to someone's garage sale and take a deduction, even if you give the proceeds to charity.

If you are audited, the IRS will demand documentation of your charitable contributions. For cash contributions you need a canceled check, a receipt from the charity, or other reliable written evidence documenting the name of the charity, the date of the contribution, and the amount of the gift. For property contributions you need a written record that includes the name of the organization, the date and value of the gift, and sufficient details to identify the property. A receipt isn't required in cases when it's impractical to obtain; for example, if you donate clothes at a charity's drop site. But the burden of proving the value, date, location, and description of the contribution is yours.

Even people who don't itemize may deduct part of their charitable contributions. For every $4 donated to charities you may deduct $1, up to a ceiling of $75 for 1984. You may deduct 50 percent of donations up to $300 in 1985 and 100 percent of your donation up to $300 in 1986.

Medical Expenses

You may deduct only the amount of medical costs that exceeds 5 percent of your adjusted gross income. You can't deduct over-the-counter drugs; only prescriptions and insulin. Other deductible medical expenses include birth control pills or other contraceptives, legal abortions, psychiatric counseling, and cosmetic surgery.

Property and Casualty Losses

When you suffer personal property loss through accident, theft, vandalism, fire, or other disasters, you may deduct part of those losses on your tax return—but only that portion of the unreimbursed loss that exceeds 10 percent of your adjusted gross income plus $100.

For example, if your adjusted gross income is $35,000, you can claim a deduction only for any unreimbursed loss exceeding $3,600 (10 percent of $35,000 plus the first $100). The limits apply to the total of your losses for the year, not just one item. You must deduct $100 of the loss for each casualty.

Energy Tax Credit

You are eligible if you install solar, wind, or geothermal energy-saving equipment such as solar heating panels in your house. You may take a credit of 40 percent of the first $10,000 spent on energy conservation in an existing or newly built house. Unless Congress extends it, this credit expires at the end of 1985. If you install energy-saving materials, such as storm doors, storm windows, or caulking, on homes completed before April 20, 1977, you can receive a tax credit of 15 percent of the first $2,000 you spend ($300 tax credit). This, too, expires at the end of 1985, unless Congress renews it. You don't have to itemize your taxes to claim the credits, just file Form 5695. *Note:* The IRS closely monitors this item.

Job-hunting Expenses

None of your expenses are deductible if you are looking for your first job or if your search doesn't result in a job. But if you are looking for a job in the same line of work you're in now you may deduct expenses such as printing and mailing your résumé, business lunches that could lead to job prospects, employment agency fees, and travel expenses. Keep good records.

Moving Expenses

When your move is job-related, you may deduct moving expenses as long as your new office is at least thirty-five miles farther from your former home than your old office. If you are unemployed and move following a job offer, your office must be at least thirty-five miles away from your former residence. To claim the deduction, you must work thirty-nine of the first fifty-two weeks following your move; if you're self-employed you must work seventy-eight weeks of the next two years.

Political Contributions

You may claim a credit for half the amount you contribute to political candidates, up to $50 on a single return or $100 on a joint return. You will need a written receipt, such as a canceled check, to document your contribution.

Miscellaneous

Don't forget to deduct these items: passport fees for a business trip, tax advice expenses and books, the cost of business and trade publications, and outstanding debts owed you.

DO-IT-YOURSELF OR HIRE AN EXPERT?

We would all prefer to pay someone else to do an onerous chore for us. Tax season may find you questioning the wisdom of preparing your own tax return rather than hiring a tax professional. There's no formula for determining when to consult an expert; even the experts disagree on this matter. Some say a professional tax preparer will always spot more ways to cut your

tax bill. Others say doing your own taxes is the best way to
understand the tax system and your own personal finances.

Consider these guidelines when you make a decision:

- Complexity of your return. If most of your income comes
  from wages, not investments, and your itemized deductions
  are common ones such as a mortgage interest, then you
  probably can handle your own taxes. Situations that generally warrant an expert's help include buying or selling a
  house or apartment, income from several sources, income
  averaging, partnership income, stocks bought on margin,
  substantial business travel or entertainment expenses not
  reimbursed by your employer, marriage or divorce, owning
  rental property, working overseas, several transactions involving capital gains and losses, tax shelter investments, and
  setting up trusts to transfer assets to a relative.
- Income. The more money you earn, the more likely you are
  to need professional help because you have the most to gain
  from each tax dollar you save. People in 40 percent or
  higher tax brackets may not have complicated returns, but
  may still need professional help to identify all the deductions
  they are eligible to take.
- Personal preferences. You may keep meticulous records and
  enjoy—or at least not abhor—doing your taxes. Or the mere
  thought of reading forms and crunching numbers may make
  you twitch and you would pay any amount to avoid it. It's
  strictly personal. Even if you do hire an expert, do your taxes
  yourself first in pencil so you know what's involved. You,
  not the preparer, are ultimately responsible for any errors
  on your return.

Once you decide to seek advice, you can choose among several
sources, depending on how much money and time you want to
spend. There are self-help tax guides, commercial tax preparation centers, accountants, lawyers, and enrolled agents. All tax

preparation expenses and fees are tax-deductible, as long as you itemize.

- Books. Bookstores and libraries are filled with books on how to do your taxes. But the best tax guides are free: the instructions that accompany your 1040 form and the Internal Revenue Service Publication 17, "Your Income Taxes," which summarize recent changes in the tax laws in understandable language. You can get the latter by writing to your local IRS Service Center (see Appendix III).
- Commercial tax preparers. If you don't need sophisticated advice, chain storefront operations such as H & R Block are a good alternative to a more costly private accountant. H & R Block, for example, typically charges about $50 to fill out a simple tax return. Drawbacks to this type of chain operation: Many tax preparers are temporary employees who don't live with and study the tax laws all year round. The advice you receive is conservative, which means that when there's a doubt the tax preparer will resolve it in favor of the IRS, not you. Private preparers tend to be more aggressive in preparing your return. If a Block employee— or some other commercial preparer—makes an error on your return, the company will pay the penalty and interest due on its discovery. If you're audited, a company employee will go to the audit free, and explain how the return was prepared.
- Accountants. All certified public accountants (CPAs) are accountants, but not all accountants are CPAs. A CPA has met certain state licensing requirements and is subject to regulation by a state board; the others aren't. Accountants' fees vary tremendously. The normal range is $100 for a simple return to $1,000 or more for a complex return that requires analysis and research. Keep good records so you don't waste professional time establishing minor points. Most accountants will represent you in a later administrative

dispute with the IRS (as long as it's not in tax court, where you must be represented by a lawyer), but expect to pay them at hourly rates starting at about $50.

- Enrolled agents. These are former IRS agents who have worked as IRS auditors for at least five years or have passed an exam given by the IRS. An enrolled agent may have a narrow scope of experience, so ask about his or her background. Enrolled agents are not always easy to find, since there are only about 20,000 of them, but start by looking for a listing in the Yellow Pages (under "Tax Return Preparation") or by writing to the professional organization (National Association of Enrolled Agents, 5410 Grosvenor Lane, Suite 140, Bethesda, MD 20814, 301-897-8702) for a referral in your area. Rates generally are more expensive than those of a commercial preparer, but cheaper than an individual CPA.

- Tax planners. When you reach a marginal tax bracket of 40 percent or higher, you may want to hire a year-round adviser such as an accountant or a financial planner to help you with long-range tax strategy and estate planning and to inform you of recent IRS and tax court rulings that affect you. You pay from $500 to $3,000 a year for these services.

- Tax lawyers. Lawyers are less likely than accountants to get involved in preparing your tax return. Lawyers, however, do have expertise in specialized areas of tax law—such as starting or liquidating a business, setting up a trust, or handling a divorce. A good one will charge you about $200 an hour, so make sure your problem requires the degree of expertise for which you will pay. Only attorneys, not CPAs or enrolled agents, may represent you in tax court.

Caveats: Steer clear of any preparer who guarantees that your return won't be audited; the IRS works in random and mysterious ways. Be suspicious of any preparer who promises you a refund without carefully studying your tax situation. It is illegal for a preparer to give you a refund immediately in return for endorsing and cashing your refund check when it arrives. Don't sign a blank tax return and leave it with the preparer. Always ask for a copy of your return and examine it carefully before you sign it.

SOURCES OF FREE TAX HELP

There is an alternative to doing your taxes yourself or hiring a tax professional: free tax advice offered by the folks who interpret and enforce the tax laws. With a staff of 1,500 full-time taxpayer service assisters and 11,000 offices, the IRS is the largest source of free taxpayer assistance in the country. Many people don't utilize these services, either because they don't know the help is available or out of paranoia. There's no reason to fear that if you ask the IRS for advice you won't be informed of all the deductions for which you are eligible or that you will be snarled up in the bureaucracy without getting an answer. The advice is not always first-rate, however, so it's wiser to use these sources only to answer basic questions.

- Toll-free hotlines. Tele-Tax is a national system of prerecorded messages on common questions regarding filing requirements and status, tax credits, and itemized deductions. Big Brother is not watching—no record is kept of your call. It may take several tries to get through during the March and April rush.
- Legal help for an audit. About thirty law and accounting schools provide free assistance if you are audited or would like to appeal an IRS ruling. Law and accounting students, who are closely supervised by professors, have the power to represent you. Accounting clinics help taxpayers prepare for audits and establish a feasible schedule for paying back taxes. The legal and accounting clinics have been judged competent to represent taxpayers by the IRS and Treasury Depart-

ment. You can call your local IRS office for a list of clinics nearest you.

- Films and speakers on tax preparation for your professional or civic group. The IRS will send an expert to lecture on any topic. And the IRS maintains a library of films available on your request.

- Seminars. If you volunteer to help others prepare their income tax returns, you are eligible for the IRS's free three-day training course in income tax preparation. You must devote twenty hours of volunteer work during tax-filing season. You don't need an accounting, law, or tax preparation background to participate. The courses are usually given during the fall, so check with your local IRS office by late summer for information (see Appendix III).

- Written assistance. If you want a detailed question answered, and a record of the answer, the IRS will respond to your tax questions in writing. Send the letter to your district office, including a complete description of any IRS employee you've dealt with previously, your phone number, address, and Social Security number. The IRS says it will answer most written requests within two weeks.

- Problem Resolution Program. This office of last resort is available when resolving the problem through normal IRS channels has failed. For example, staffers can help you with problems concerning missing refund checks, lost forms, and the status of an audit. The program operates out of every district and regional IRS office and in the ten IRS service centers.

SURVIVING AN AUDIT

An audit notice evokes universal fear, even when you have done nothing illegal and have documentation to back up the deductions claimed. The fear is rooted in the belief that the IRS is questioning your integrity (it is); that the government is intruding further into your life; and that you might have to pay more tax money and stiff late penalties.

Statistically, your chances of an audit are slight. Overall, only 1.5 percent of taxpayers are audited in any one year, but your chances of being one of the chosen few increase with your income. Of those who earn between $25,000 and $50,000 a year, 2.6 percent are audited; of those who earn over $50,000 a year, almost 5 percent are audited. There is absolutely no way to guard against an audit. Yes, there is a general consensus among former tax agents and experienced accountants about red flags—certain deductions guaranteed to set off alarms at the IRS and bring an auditor to your door. Red flags are not the only audit triggers, though. The IRS randomly chooses about 55,000 taxpayers every three years to monitor taxpayer compliance. The survey, called the Taxpayer Compliance Measurement Program, is designed to gather facts to determine the average amount of deductions, exemptions, losses, and credits that taxpayers at various income levels pay.

The IRS then uses the survey to come up with a formula based partly on the amount of deductions you take in relation to your income. Generally, if your return doesn't jibe with this formula, a giant IRS computer will kick it out as a candidate for an audit. Then a person, not a computer, determines if your return is worth auditing.

The IRS has three years from the date the return was due or filed, whichever was later, to challenge your return. In cases of suspected fraud, there is no time limit.

Here are items that tax experts say are most likely to trigger an audit of your return:

- Loss from a tax shelter. The IRS has been waging a well-publicized campaign against "abusive" tax shelters. "Abusive" generally means investments that don't make much economic sense and use as their main selling point a promise of big reductions in current taxes.

- Excessive personal deductions. For example, "excessive" generally means charitable contributions that are high in proportion to your income, casualty losses over $500, and interest payments to family members. The more deductions you take, the more likely the IRS is to take an interest in your return.

- Sloppy return. When the IRS receives your return it is entered into a computer and the math is checked for accuracy. Errors increase the probability of an audit, as does a return riddled with erasures and crossed-out lines. The IRS is likely to think that a sloppy return indicates sloppy records and it will be easy to assess you for more taxes. Tip: Do your return in pencil, then photocopy it and send it in.

- Increase in exemptions. The IRS takes a keen interest if the number of exemptions you claim takes a sharp jump from year to year.

- Hobby losses. These refer to losses from activities such as stamp collecting or horse breeding that you don't necessarily practice for profit.

- The wrong tax preparer. If you hire a tax preparer whom the IRS suspects of fraudulent or careless work, the agency may pull and scrutinize the returns of all his or her clients in a given year.

- Certain occupations. Anyone with substantial travel, business, and entertainment expenses has a higher probability of being audited. This includes professionals such as doctors, dentists, salespeople, stockbrokers, airline pilots, and the media.

- The self-employed. Owners of businesses that deal in cash, especially those with complicated tax returns, interest the IRS because of the many opportunities for unreported income.

- People with high incomes. They generally have more tax shelters, deductions, and investments that interest the tax collectors. Auditors can collect more money from people in the highest tax brackets because more of every dollar they earn is taxed. Taxpayers reporting $50,000 or more in wages, interest, dividends, and other ventures are in the high risk group.

- Home office deduction. Although the IRS is slacking off in this area lately, it still elicits interest from auditors. Your business doesn't have to be a full-time activity. To deduct part of your home as an office, however, you must use it as the principal place of business; or as a place to meet with clients, customers, or patients; or for the convenience of your employer.
- Tax protesters. The best way to get audited is to write "I protest" on your tax form and refuse to pay your taxes.

Many taxpayers react to any request from the IRS for more information as an audit. It isn't, as Sue and Paul learned when they called their uncle, an experienced accountant. What they had received was a simple computerized request for additional information, which is smaller in scope than an audit.

In any case, whether you receive a request for more information or a formal audit notice, there are ways to minimize your trauma. Your strongest line of defense is to keep meticulous records. (Refer to Chapter 1 for advice on setting up a record-keeping system for taxes.) The minimum number of separate files you should keep for tax purposes are for income records, canceled checks, interest deductions, investments, medical expenses, sales slips, housing expenses, and unreimbursed business expenses.

If you are notified of an audit, get it over with as soon as possible. There's no problem if you must delay it for a valid reason such as an out-of-town business trip or a personal emergency. If the agent thinks you are just stalling, however, he or she may be suspicious of your motives. Don't try to change the location of an audit if it's scheduled for the IRS office. Reason: The IRS sends out a higher-level agent if an audit takes place at your house or office or in your accountant's or lawyer's office.

Prepare for the audit in advance as if you are going to an exam.

You are. For example, if you have claimed medical expenses, type up a schedule listing the expenses, and take canceled checks along to back up your claims. Don't walk in with a disorganized pile of papers in a shoebox. Some preparers specialize in helping you get organized for an audit.

Unless your audit notice is simple and focuses on a narrow area such as your mortgage deduction or your interest and dividends, hire a tax expert to go to the audit in your place. If the audit notice is simple, but you talk incessantly under stress, then hire a tax professional to go instead of you.

When you are there, respond only to the specific question. Additional information you offer innocently could lead to trouble. Never use the excuse that everyone else does it if a deduction is questioned because the agent may ask you to name names. Don't feel compelled to answer questions if you don't know the answer. There is nothing wrong with saying you'll look it up and get back to the agent.

Dress for the audit in clothes you wear to the office. Don't try to look too rich or too poor; it will only irritate the agent, who will see through any obvious tricks. Don't vent hostility on the agent—the agent wants to get the job done as pleasantly as possible.

By all means, hire a professional representative—a lawyer, certified public accountant, or an enrolled agent—if the audit involves an unusual transaction such as a tax shelter partnership. Be wary if the IRS asks for all your bank receipts for a year or so. It indicates a significant examination and you'll need expert advice.

Alone with the IRS agent, your tax professional can negotiate on your behalf, peer to peer. But the agent is unlikely to make any concessions with you there as a witness.

Sue and Paul walked out of their meeting with the IRS smiling. "Let's call Uncle Jerry. I can't wait to tell him that the IRS owes us $36.24," Sue said.

Uncle Jerry's advice had been simple: take only the records that were requested, nothing else. Answer all questions specifically. Type up a schedule listing all the business expenses claimed and bring in canceled checks to back up the claims.

Sue and Paul had brought a typed list of their business expenses: subscriptions for professional journals and magazines, and work-related entertainment costs. They had receipts for most of the expenditures.

The IRS agent, who looked a few years younger than they were, wasn't an ogre. In fact, he pointed out they had made an arithmetic error. They were entitled to $36.24 more than they had claimed. He told them which form to file to collect it.

"I promise I'll never accuse you of being overcompulsive about keeping tax records," Sue told Paul. "You saved us."

"You know I don't like to say I told you so," Paul replied.

3

INSURANCE

TOM THOUGHT HE RECOGNIZED THE GUY STANDING across from him in the locker room, the one who was staring at him.

"Hey, you're Tom Garfield, aren't you? Remember me? I'm Joe Silver. We belonged to the same fraternity. You were a year ahead of me."

"Yes, I remember you. You used to date Elizabeth Brown. What are you doing these days?"

"I'm the vice president of an insurance agency here in town."

Tom was sorry he had asked. He considered telling Joe he had an incurable disease.

"How about a game of squash? We can catch up as we play," Joe asked.

Here comes the hard sell, Tom thought. He might as well get it over with.

As he showered after the game, Tom thought over what Joe had told him. He knew it was Joe's job to sell insurance, but maybe it did make sense to buy a whole life policy. If he waited another five or ten years it would cost a lot more, Joe said. In the meantime, the cash value of the policy would grow. After all, Tom knew he wasn't doing a good job saving on his own.

But didn't he already get free life insurance coverage from work? Tom thought he remembered naming his younger brother as his beneficiary on some personnel forms. He would have to check.

"Tom, thanks for the game. It was a good workout," Joe yelled. "I'll call you next week."

"Okay. Speak to you soon. My best to Elizabeth."

Ellen unlocked the door to the apartment. "Oh, no," she said. "Hurry up, Scott. We've been robbed."

The thief had entered by smashing the window next to the fire escape and then climbing through. Clothes, books, and records were scattered on the living room floor. The *TV Guide* was sitting on the armchair; the three-year-old color television set was gone. The kitchen cabinets were open; the stainless steel flatware was there, but not the food processor. In the bedroom, what was left of Ellen's jewelry had been dumped on the bed. Missing were her pearls, a gold chain, and the antique diamond ring she had inherited from her aunt.

Scott opened the hall closet and discovered his luggage was missing. "The thief probably used it to carry out the loot," he said.

Ellen sat on the floor and wept. "Why us? We didn't have much. I told you we needed a bar on that window."

"Ellen, don't cry. They were only material things. But my stereo was my favorite thing in the world."

"At least we're covered by my insurance," Ellen said.

They would find out soon enough that she was only half right.

LIFE INSURANCE

Insurance is not an investment. It's a gamble; a gamble that you will die sooner rather than later; that your house will be ripped off; that your new Porsche will be stolen from the lot. You buy insurance as a hedge to cover your bets and to minimize your losses in case something bad does happen.

After checking his benefits at work, Tom learned he was covered by a $100,000 policy. The beneficiary was his brother Jeff, the corporate lawyer. Tom just didn't need an extra policy. He wasn't supporting anyone except himself, and his policy would adequately cover any costs arising from his death.

When they met for lunch later that week, Tom told Joe that he didn't need extra insurance now. But if his needs changed—for instance, when he married and had children—he would call him.

Joe's sales pitch to Tom had emphasized these points:

- It would be cheaper and easier for Tom to buy a whole life policy now. In ten years or so, it would be tougher to pass the physical required before a policy is issued. In fact, that isn't true.
- A whole life policy would give Tom a form of enforced savings. The premiums he paid in over a lifetime would accumulate with tax-free interest until withdrawn.

True enough, but these issues overlooked the most important element: need. Tom—and other single young professionals—don't need life insurance because nobody depends on their income. It's that simple. What's more, many employers provide life insurance, enough to settle your estate and pay your burial costs.

When you marry, or have children, reevaluate your needs. For example, if Tom were married, had a child, his wife didn't work, and his company didn't provide much insurance, the scenario would be different. Then Tom might want more insurance. Let's take a look at the factors that would influence his decision.

Although the insurance industry thrives on creating and selling complicated products, basically there are only two types: term and whole life. All other products are variations on these two. We will focus our discussion on them.

Term Insurance

Term insurance policies offer pure insurance protection. You buy a fixed amount of protection at a predetermined price for a limited amount of time. If you die during that time, the insurer will pay your beneficiary. Most term policies are renewable when they run out, but you pay more money for premiums each year. Reason: As you grow older your chance of dying increases. Most insurance companies will not sell you a new term policy after you reach age 70.

At age 29 Tom, who doesn't smoke (smokers pay 12 percent to 15 percent more for most policies), could expect to pay about $170 a year for a $100,000 term policy, renewable each year. At age 39 he could expect to pay about $225 annually; at age 49, $525 annually; at age 59, $1,355 annually; at ages 65 through 70, $2,445 a year; and at age 70, $4,320 a year. After that, the insurer wouldn't sell him more coverage.

For young professionals starting out, my advice is stick to term. It offers the most protection for the least cost. Term policies are straightforward, and you can figure out how much of the premium goes to sales charges and commissions without taking advanced accounting classes. Term has no savings component, so you don't have to worry about figuring out the rate of return.

Don't be swayed if you want to buy term insurance but your insurance agent tries to talk you into whole life. Insurance agents earn higher commissions on whole life. The agent typically receives a first-year commission equal to 50 percent to 100 percent of the premium; then receives a 9 percent commission in years two and three; a 7 percent commission in years four and five; a 5 percent commission in years six through ten; and a 3 percent commission thereafter. On a term policy, an agent typically receives a 35 to 65 percent commission on the much lower premium (than whole life) the first year; a 10 percent commission in years two and three; an 8 percent commission in years four and five; a 5 percent commission in years six through ten; and 2 to 3 percent thereafter.

When you buy term insurance, buy it from a company that allows you to convert it to whole life, in case you want to switch later. Most companies provide this option. Don't buy any life insurance based on price alone. You want the company to be solvent when it's time to collect benefits. Check "Best's Insurance Reports (Life-Health)," published annually by A.M. Best & Co., and available in most public libraries. It rates insurers on financial strength, grading them from A+ to C. Choose an insurer from the A+ or A category.

Whole Life

Whole life—also called "ordinary life," or "straight life"—combines insurance protection and a tax-deferred savings plan. Unlike term, you're covered for your entire life as long as you keep paying the premiums, which typically end when you reach age 65. You pay the same amount for premiums during your lifetime, but the premiums start out about six times higher than term. With whole life, the amount you pay in when you are younger subsidizes the amount you pay later. The extra money you contribute in the early years is invested and builds up a cash value in your policy. As your savings grow, the amount of insurance protection you get shrinks. When you die, the insurer pays out the face amount of the policy.

For example, if Tom, at age 29, bought a whole life policy offered by one large insurer, he would pay $1,200 a year for a $100,000 policy. Because his insurer is a "mutual" company owned by its policyholders rather than a "stock" company, he would get a dividend refund each year. Why? Stock companies are owned by shareholders and are supposed to make a profit. Only stockholders get dividends, not policyholders. Mutual companies are owned by the policyholders and some of their premium is returned each year in the form of dividends.

Tom could use the refund to reduce his premium payments or to increase his coverage. The interest rate he receives on the cash value of his policy is currently 10.75 percent. (The industry range is 4 to 12 percent, tax-deferred, depending on the insurer.) Company fees are subtracted before interest is paid to the policyholders.

If Tom uses his dividends to buy more coverage, then at age 65 he would stop making payments and have $395,000 of insurance protection for the rest of his life. Or Tom could convert his policy into an **annuity**, which is a plan that provides you with income for the rest of your life. Many life insurance policies can be turned into an annuity when you retire. After 36 years of paying $1,200 premiums (assuming an interest rate of roughly 11 percent), the annuity would pay close to $27,000 a year or $2,250 a month (before taxes) for life.

It sounds like Tom can't lose. That's a lot of money. Think again. If inflation averaged 6 percent a year, that $2,250 is $300 in today's dollars—peanuts. The money he earns in interest on the cash value of his policy is not taxed as it mounts up. But when Tom cashed in the policy he would pay taxes on the difference between the amount he paid in and what he received.

Whole life does have its advantages. You can use it to raise cash in an emergency; you can't with term. The reason is that you can borrow on the cash value of a policy at rates below the personal loan rate from banks or other lenders. When you borrow, you don't even have to repay the loan. If you die before you repay it, the insurance company will subtract what you owe and any unpaid interest from the amount it pays your beneficiaries.

Still, those advantages don't outweigh a major disadvantage: If you drop your policy after several years you will get back less than you contributed. For example, if Tom couldn't keep up his premiums after five years and $5,450 paid in, he could:

- Take the policy's cash value of $3,500, incurring a $1,950 loss.
- Convert the $3,500 into a fully paid-up $13,000 whole life policy, which would be paid to his beneficiary whenever he died.
- Convert the $3,500 into a $100,000 term policy for as long as it would last—in this case, about ten years.

To sum up, whole life is not a good investment for young professionals. It makes more sense to buy term, which is straight insurance coverage, and invest the difference yourself in other ways. Traditionally, the savings portion of whole life policies has earned very low rates of return compared to other investment products. And there's a risk that you may be forced to drop your policy after a few years, which could cause you to lose money.

Universal Life

Universal life, a variation of whole life, deserves a passing mention. Introduced in 1980, it has become popular because it's far more flexible than ordinary whole life.

The cash value of the policy rises and falls according to the investment success of the insurer. Universal life allows you to mix and match the elements of term life insurance and a tax-deferred savings plan. For example, you may increase or decrease the size of your premium year to year; raise and lower coverage limits; vary the distribution of the premium between pure insurance protection and the investment portion, and withdraw money from the savings portion of the policy without paying stiff penalties or canceling your insurance coverage.

At times of high interest rates, universal policies can pay attractive rates, as much as triple that of whole-life policies. But do you want insurance or an investment?

If you're looking for the best insurance buy, term is better because you will pay for the flexibility and high interest rates universal policies allow. For example, the term insurance portion of universal may be more expensive than regular term insurance, and if interest rates are low the savings portion won't make up for it. Also, high first-year charges and annual service fees reduce your yield considerably on many policies.

DISABILITY INSURANCE

Many young professionals buy more life insurance than they need but make the mistake of not buying enough individual disability insurance. Your earning potential is your most valuable asset and must be protected. A serious illness or accident could cut off your stream of income for several years and leave you in terrible financial shape.

Don't assume Social Security benefits will cover all disability expenses. They won't. While Social Security provides disability insurance if your disability is expected to last longer than one year or result in death, payments may be too little, too late. The maximum monthly benefits paid in 1985 are $872 at age 25, $796 at age 35, and $749 at age 45.

Of course, if your company provides it, you won't need extra disability insurance. Review your coverage when you switch jobs because your new company may not offer it. But look for gaps in your coverage. For example, your company policy may cover only a disability that occurred at your office, or cover a shorter time than you would miss from work, or pay fewer benefits than you need to live on. Figure that you will need enough money to replace 50 to 60 percent of your gross salary if you are disabled. Integrate any new policy with your company plan. If your company covers you for one year from the time of the disability, buy a policy that starts when your company's coverage ends.

There is a maximum limit on disability coverage, usually 65 to 85 percent of your gross income. Generally, women pay more for disability coverage, which insurers justify by saying women live longer and thus have more opportunity to collect.

A few companies offer unisex rates. Under one, a 28-year-old manager earning $30,000 a year would pay premiums of $250 to $400 a year for a maximum monthly benefit ranging from $1,100 to $1,700. The policy has a six-month "elimination period"—the time you must wait from your injury until you collect benefits—and coverage until age 65.

The annual premium costs and maximum coverage vary according to your age, occupation, sex, and the individual policy, so shop around for the best rate. Buy a non-cancelable, guaranteed renewable policy so you can be covered until age 65 (some are valid until 72 or even 80). If you—not your employer or your union—pay the premiums, then any benefits you collect will be tax-free, as long as you don't deduct the premiums from your income taxes.

Read the policy provisions carefully. They are tricky. An insurer may say you are not disabled if you can work at any job (supermarket cashier, for example), even one that pays much less than your current job. Make sure the definition of disability relates to your "own occupation" rather than "any occupation" and that you can collect benefits if you're unable to perform the "material" or important duties of your job. Some policies state that if you can perform any duty (i.e., getting coffee), then you are not disabled. To avoid problems later, ask the insurance company for a written definition of "disability" and who determines it—your doctor or theirs. Naturally, you prefer your own doctor.

A long elimination period will save you money, so figure out how long you can last—using up sick leave, vacation, or savings—before collecting. Buy coverage that will pay benefits until age 65 when Social Security retirement payments begin. It is risky to buy less coverage and extremely expensive to buy coverage beyond age 65.

AUTOMOBILE INSURANCE

When you buy car insurance, you buy a package of coverages including:

- Bodily injury liability, which covers lawyers' costs and claims for injuries by you or your car's driver. It also covers you and family members living with you for accidents when they drive someone else's car. This is the most important part of your insurance.
- Property damage liability covers you if you harm someone else's property or car.

- Medical payments coverage takes care of medical expenses caused by you or another driver driving your car or if you or family members are hit by a car when walking. Most people don't need this coverage because it overlaps with their medical insurance benefits, so if you have good medical insurance you can skip it.
- Collision. If you hit something, this type of coverage pays for damage to your car that exceeds the deductible amount, no matter who's at fault. If you have an old car you probably don't need it.
- Comprehensive covers you for losses not caused by collision —fire, glass breakage, hail, flood, or if your car is damaged, stolen, or vandalized. It's often sold with a $50 to $250 deductible.
- Uninsured motorist coverage protects you and passengers in your car for injuries caused by an uninsured or a hit-and-run driver, as long as it's the other person's fault.
- No-fault insurance laws, adopted by many states, mean bodily injury claims are paid by the injured person's own insurance company, not the other person's.

How Much You Need

Don't buy too much physical damage coverage and don't skimp on liability insurance. Insure against major catastrophes that would wipe you out financially, not small losses—scratches in the parking garage—that you can afford to absorb.

If your car is older than four years, consider skipping collision and comprehensive coverage. Weigh the costs of buying a new or used car versus the cost of repair after a collision. You may be better off foregoing the insurance and putting the premium money in the bank, just in case.

If your car is new or you want to buy physical damage insurance anyway, take the highest deductible you can afford, at least $250 to $500, or an amount equal to your weekly net paycheck. A $500 deductible cuts the premium by about 50 percent.

If you are willing to pay higher premium prices, some insurers offer replacement cost insurance, which covers the amount you'd need to buy a new car or a newer one if your car is wrecked beyond the reasonable cost of repair.

Many states require you to buy a minimum of $25,000 to $50,000 of personal liability insurance. But the minimum probably isn't enough. You can increase your coverage to $100,000 at a minimal cost. The price varies by state depending on such factors as where you live, your sex, your age, type of car, and how many miles you drive a year.

Keeping Auto Premium Costs Down

The cost of your auto insurance premiums depends on your age, sex, where you live and work, what model car you drive, your driving record, and the insurer. Finding the best rate means calling around, unless your state insurance department publishes a consumer guide. For example, New York, Connecticut, Florida, and Virginia are among those that do. Before you buy a policy, check the company's financial stability in "Best's Insurance Reports (Property—Casualty)," available at local libraries. Buy insurance only from companies with an excellent (A or A+) rating.

Here are tips for saving money on your automobile premiums:

- When shopping for a car, consider the repair costs. The higher the repair costs, the higher your insurance rates.
- Don't ignore the impact a Corvette or Porsche will have on insurance rates, especially if you are a single man under age twenty-five. Some insurance companies refuse to write policies on certain models because they are stolen so often, so check with your insurer before you buy the car.
- Ask about discounts you may be eligible to get for maintaining a clean driving record with one insurer for five years, for nonsmokers, for driving a conservative model car, for carpooling, and for single women, ages 30 to 64, who are the sole drivers in their household.

- If you marry and each have a car, buy one insurance policy to cover both cars. A multiple car discount could cut your overall rate up to 25 percent.
- If you live with someone and share one or more cars, both of your names should be listed on each policy to avoid disputes over who's responsible if an accident occurs.

HEALTH INSURANCE

You probably don't need health insurance because you are covered free or at low rates through an employer's group health plan. Frequently, your employer will ask you to choose between a Health Maintenance Organization (HMO) and the traditional group medical insurance.

The HMO is a prepaid plan, which means you or your employer pay a fixed monthly fee for unlimited health care: checkups, laboratory tests, prescription drugs, and additional office visits.

Under the traditional health insurance plan, you pay the bills until they exceed your deductible. Then you pay a fixed percentage (typically 20 percent) of the total expenses; your employer pays the rest. These plans place an annual dollar limit on coverage.

Consider these questions when choosing between an HMO and group medical insurance:

- How much choice do you want in selecting your doctor and the location of your medical care?

  In an HMO, you choose a "primary care physician," responsible for coordinating your medical treatment. The type of HMO determines your range of choices. With a staff model, the physicians are on salary and housed under one roof. In a medical group model, doctors with a group practice divide their time between HMO members and private patients. With an individual practice association, doctors affiliate with an HMO; you choose one and go to the doctor's office for treatment (where private patients are also treated). You have the widest selection of doctors with an individual practice association; the least choice with a staff model HMO.

A major medical insurance plan does not limit you to preselected doctors. If you recently moved to a community and do not know how to choose doctors, though, an HMO gives you instant access to the medical system.

- Are the HMO's health centers or doctors' offices convenient to where you live or work?

Do you prefer a "one-stop shopping" HMO where the doctors, laboratories, and your medical records are at one site? Of course, if the HMO is in an inconvenient neighborhood, it's not worth the hassle.

- Are you comfortable with the level of personal care available?

Some patients feel that an HMO is impersonal and you will not get the same attention you get from a private doctor. A private doctor has a financial incentive to cater to the patient even when the problem isn't that serious; the HMO doctor has no incentive to give you unnecessary medical tests or treatments. If you don't like the service you receive from your doctor, at an HMO or in private practice, select another one. Don't let the fear of impersonal service sway you.

- Are you willing to risk out-of-pocket expenses if an unexpected medical problem arises?

Under a medical insurance plan you can't predict your expenses. Often there's a time lag between paying the doctors' bills and collecting the claims, and you have to lay out the cash. With an HMO, there are no surprises.

- Are you bothered by the paperwork requirements of processing insurance claims?

Once your HMO's fees are paid, you do not have to pay bills or fill out claim forms.

- How long will you have to wait for an appointment?

Find out the typical waiting time for eye and gynecological examinations, and how long you'll wait when you get there.

- Is twenty-four-hour access important to you?

HMOs are required by law to provide twenty-four-hour emergency services; many private doctors are not so accessible.

- Are more of the medical services that you anticipate needing covered under one type of plan?

For example, if you are interested in mental health care or maternity benefits, choose a plan based on those needs.

Married people should integrate health insurance coverage with their spouse. For example, if you both must pay for individual coverage from your employers, it's probably cheaper to switch to family coverage on the better of the two plans and drop the other.

If you are not covered by a group plan, buying health insurance on your own is expensive. It's cheaper to join a group plan through a professional association or an HMO as an individual. For more information about HMO membership, write to: Group Health Association of America, 624 9th Street, NW, Washington, DC 20001.

If you can't get group or HMO coverage, seek the help of an agent experienced in shopping for health insurance. Comparisons in costs and coverages are too baffling for a novice to brave alone. Buy a non-cancelable, guaranteed renewable policy; as you get older you are bound to develop medical conditions that will make coverage tougher to find and more expensive. Buy the highest deductible you can afford to keep your rates down.

HOMEOWNER'S INSURANCE

Ellen hung up after speaking to her insurance agent, wondering how to tell Scott the bad news. Her personal property coverage for $10,000 didn't mean that all the items in their apartment were insured up to $10,000—only her belongings were insured. They wouldn't collect a penny for Scott's stereo set, luggage, or food processor.

Even her own coverage wasn't complete. The color television set from her parents would cost $500 to replace. But the claim settlement would be only $250: $350 for the three-year-old set minus the $100 deductible. But they couldn't afford to replace the TV. Instead, they could put the $250 toward a new stereo, but it would probably take years to save enough for the rest of it.

More bad news about the jewelry. She had never read the fine print. The maximum limit for her total jewelry losses was $500. Just replacing the pearls would cost that much.

Whether you rent or own, you need homeowner's insurance. It protects your property against loss or damage from theft, natural disasters, vandalism, and other perils. Also, if someone is hurt on your property, you are protected should the individual claim damages. As a renter, you would not be held responsible if someone was hurt on the property unless you caused the accident—for example, if you dropped a soup pot and scalded a dinner guest.

Insurers offer homeowner's plans numbered HO-1 to HO-8. The most popular coverage for homeowners is HO-3. Renters and cooperative apartment owners need an HO-4 policy; condominium unit owners would buy an HO-6 policy. Each policy has a deductible clause, typically $100 and $250. You can pick supplemental insurance according to your own needs, which are often determined by your type of housing.

Condo owners should coordinate individual policies with the building's master policy to prevent gaps and overlaps. The master policy, owned by the condo association, normally protects common areas such as hallways and parking lots. Make sure you understand specifics of where your personal coverage starts and the master policy ends. For instance, if a fire damages the living room wallpaper, who pays to replace it—you or the condo association?

There are two types of condominium insurance—"single entity" and "barewall." With single entity, the unit owner must insure only personal property inside the unit and additions or alterations made to the original structure; the condo association insures the unit the way it was built, including items such as the cabinets and kitchen stove. But most condominiums have barewall protection, which means the unit owner is responsible for insuring fixtures, built-in appliances, wiring, plumbing, paint, floor coverings, and tiles, as well as personal possessions.

If you own a co-op, a tenant's insurance policy provides basic coverage for your personal property and liability to others.

When you insure your house, the amount you buy governs the amount of insurance on the rest of your property. For example, if you insure your house for $100,000, half of that, or $50,000, will apply to the contents of the house and other personal property on the premises. There are limits, however, on certain items such as jewelry or furs, but these limits can be raised by buying extra coverage. This supplement to your basic policy is called a **personal articles floater**. An **endorsement** is a form, attached to an insurance policy to add or alter its provisions, which tells you what is and isn't covered.

Renters determine their own contents coverage, but the minimum amount is usually $6,000—and it may be as high as $15,000. The personal liability minimum is usually $25,000 for renters, but higher if you own a home. The majority (about 75 percent) of renters carry no homeowner's insurance at all. Others, like Ellen and Scott, wrongly assume they have ample protection—until they want to collect it.

Renters who live together need two separate policies. Cohabitants living in a house, condo, or co-op owned jointly or by one of them need only one policy because the policy protects the property, not the individuals. Both names should be listed on the policy to protect their separate interests.

If you sublet a house or condo or co-op, the owner should have insurance to protect the structure or unit. But you still need renter's insurance to protect your own belongings.

Newly married couples, whether they rent or own, should reevaluate their insurance needs. After their wedding, Sue and Paul didn't have enough insurance to protect their new wedding rings, antique clock, crystal, and china. Each $1,000 worth of extra coverage costs about $12 or less a year. Newlyweds should add their gifts to their household inventories.

These key phrases will help you understand your policy:

- Actual cash value. You would collect an amount equal to the current replacement cost of the item minus depreciation.
- Replacement cost coverage (also called "insuring to value"). If you pay about 30 percent to 40 percent more for premiums, many companies will insure you for the full cost of replacing an item, without docking you for depreciation.
- Inflation guard. Many policies are written to automatically increase your coverage every few months to adjust for inflation.

Even with inflation guards, there are standard maximum limits for jewelry, silverware, or personal computers. For example, standard limits on a jewelry loss are $500 to $1,000 for the total loss, not for each bracelet or ring. You can buy personal articles floaters to increase your coverage of specific items or pay extra to upgrade your total coverage.

Collecting the maximum amount from the insurer depends on your records. Don't rely on memory to recall the contents of your home after it has been emptied by theft or fire. Keep a list of your belongings, containing prices and dates of purchase or acquisition, in a safe deposit box and file one copy with your insurance agent. An inventory will speed the claims process.

Update the list at least once a year, including the date you bought the new item and its replacement cost. Supplement the inventory with photographs of your rooms and valuables.

You'll need a receipt or appraisal slip to prove the value if you file a claim. With a standard homeowner's policy, your cash settlement will be based on the item's value minus depreciation minus the amount of your deductible.

Keeping Homeowner's Premium Costs Down

How much you pay for premiums depends on the insurer, whether you live in a city or suburb, when your home was built, and the crime rate in your neighborhood, among other factors. To buy the most protection for your money:

- Use the highest deductible you can afford—while $100 is standard, $250 could cut premium costs by 10 percent or more.
- The limits on your policy should match the current cost of rebuilding your home (excluding the value of the land and foundation). Homeowners shouldn't insure the value of the land and foundation because a fire (covered under a basic policy) won't destroy them. For example, if your home is valued at $100,000, and the land and foundation are worth $30,000, insure your home for a maximum of $70,000. Flood insurance isn't covered under a standard policy; you must buy it separately.
- The insurer will not reimburse you fully unless you buy a policy with coverage equal to at least 80 percent of the replacement cost of the house, not 80 percent of the market value. Buy less coverage and you'll receive money for only a portion of your loss. As your home appreciates you must raise your insurance coverage to meet the 80 percent requirement. Reappraise your house once a year—or at least every other year—to adjust for inflation and any improvements or additions.

- You can get a discount for installing smoke or burglar alarms in your house or apartment.
- When you are comparing premium costs, include extra charges for floaters and endorsements, not just the basic premium.

UMBRELLA COVERAGE

When somebody slips on your icy front steps or gets whiplash when your car skids into his car, his pain and injuries may depend on how rich he thinks you are. Insurance agents often advise doctors, lawyers, and others in highly paid professions to buy extra personal liability coverage, called "umbrellas," for protection against a disastrous lawsuit. Umbrella policies—so-called because they serve as a shelter over and above your other insurance policies—are usually issued with a minimum limit of $1 million. The coverage pays for liability claims and legal fees that exceed the limits of your auto and homeowner's policies, so you must meet the maximums on those policies first. Umbrella insurance also protects you in situations that are not always covered by standard liability policies.

The likelihood of getting sued for a catastrophic liability claim is small. But if you have large assets to protect, you may sleep better after spending the extra $85 to $100 a year for a $1 million policy.

4

CREDIT

RACHEL AND HER FRIEND ELISSA WERE SHOPPING FOR furniture. Or rather, Elissa was shopping for a couch and Rachel was along for fun. Rachel would have loved to buy a new couch herself, but she had resolved not to make any major purchases until she paid off the balance on her Master-Card. It seemed that she had been paying off the same bill forever, which wasn't technically true. But making monthly payments of $50 didn't go far toward retiring her debt when the interest charge was 20 percent.

Finally, her debt became a manageable $350.

"Look at this sofa bed. It's marked down $300. I really like it," Rachel said.

"I thought you couldn't afford anything today," Elissa reminded her.

"You know, it would really look great in my living room," Rachel said. "And it might not be on sale when I can afford it. What do you think?"

"I think we should go eat lunch now," said Elissa, steering Rachel out of the store. "If you still want to buy it later, we can come back."

Scott waited impatiently for the sales clerk to find the manager to approve his check. At last she returned with his gloves.

"Sir, if you shop here often maybe you'd like to open a charge account."

Scott picked up an application form on his way out, filled it out, sent it in, and forgot about it for a few weeks. He then received a letter, informing him, to his great surprise, that he couldn't open a charge account.

"Thank you for your recent request for credit," the letter said. "You have been turned down because of unfavorable information received by a credit reporting agency."

"I can't understand this. I pay all my debts, except for the ones to my family," he told Ellen, outraged that anyone dared impugn his integrity. "I'm never going to buy anything there again. You shouldn't either."

"Why not? I have a charge account there," Ellen said. "Why don't you write for a copy of your credit file and find out about the blot on your record?"

"That's a good idea. It's probably a mistake and I can correct it. Unless my brother wrote a letter saying that I've owed him $150 since ninth grade."

Scott glanced at the letter again, noting that it told him where to write to get a copy of his credit file.

Tom paced his apartment. "Why did my car have to die on me today? I can't get to work without a car. How can I buy a new one? My life savings amount to $823."

"Look, that car was eleven years old. You got a lot of use out of it," replied his cousin Ira, who had the misfortune to be visiting him during this crisis. "You can use your savings as a down payment and buy a used car."

"I don't want a used car. I don't want someone else's headaches. I have my own."

"You can't afford a new car. Why don't we go out to some car dealers and see what's on the lots? We can use my car to get there," Ira suggested. "There's no point in crying over a dead car, especially one that you drove over 200,000 miles. It deserved a rest."

Tom put on his coat. "I can't believe it finally died. What am I going to do now?"

YOUR CREDIT RATING

Establishing a good credit rating is essential for young professionals. Credit is a convenience as well as a necessity, enabling you to charge items in stores and restaurants, reserve hotel rooms, rent cars on business trips and vacations, and borrow money for major purchases. Lenders determine your credit-worthiness by your ability to pay back a loan (your income) and your willingness to repay it (your credit history).

Start building your credit history at a bank by opening a checking account, preferably one with "overdraft" privileges. It serves as an automatic loan covered by the bank in case you overdraw your account. The service is free, but be careful. When you use the overdraft privilege, an interest rate will be applied. And some banks will only cover the overdraft in multiples of $100, so you could end up paying interest on a higher amount than you need. But as long as you repay the debt promptly, this account will help your credit rating. Opening a savings account will help, too, but you may prefer to keep your savings in a higher-yielding bank deposit account or a money market mutual fund. Bank fees on small savings accounts (under $1,000) can wipe out any interest gains.

Using cards with "revolving" credit, such as Visa, Master-Card, and department store cards, builds your credit history, too. With a revolving credit card you can pay a fraction of your bills each month and extend your payments indefinitely, although it's not a smart habit to get into—you can easily fall into debt. Travel and entertainment cards, such as American Express and Diner's Club, and some oil company cards, are considered charge cards, not credit cards, and don't offer revolving credit. Using them won't build your credit history because those companies don't report to a credit bureau.

The annual fees and charges vary greatly on a Visa and MasterCard, depending on the issuing bank, so shop around for the best deal. You're not limited to local banks. You don't have to live in a bank's geographic area or have a checking or savings account at an institution to get a bank card. You can apply for it by mail.

Annual card fees generally range from $15 to $20, but a bank may waive the fee if you keep a minimum balance in your checking account. Steer clear of banks that charge low annual interest rates but tack on a transaction fee; for example, 12 cents for each credit card purchase. Finance charges generally vary from 18 percent to 25 percent, but some banks charge interest from the day a purchase is recorded, allowing no grace period, which will cost you more. Look for special offers. Many banks offer credit cards as package deals with other services—for instance, cash advances through automated teller machines, overdraft protection, commission-free travelers' checks, and travelers' insurance. Credit limits also vary.

If your job and credit history are short, it may be easier to get a bank card than a travel and entertainment card because minimum income requirements are generally lower. Each bank sets it own credit standards, so if one bank turns you down for a card, apply at another bank.

If you are working at your first job, you may have trouble qualifying for a national credit card such as MasterCard or Visa. But American Express has a program for college seniors and recent graduates, who can get the card by proving they have a "career-oriented" job that pays $10,000 or more a year. One drawback: The card has a high ($35) annual fee.

Another method for building your credit is to open an account at a local department store, which often will have lower credit standards than national companies. Consistent use of your charge account, along with prompt repayment of the bills, will help you establish good credit.

Should department stores turn you down, you can establish credit by taking out a small installment loan from a bank, depositing it in a savings account, and repaying the loan in fixed monthly amounts. Use this method as a last resort because it will cost you interest on the loan.

Rachel's decision regarding the couch came down to this: Any savings from buying the couch on sale would vanish when she charged an additional $700 (the sale price of the couch) on her bank card. The reason: She didn't have the money to pay off the couch in a month or two, thus the 20 percent interest costs would counteract most of the savings on the couch.

Rachel made the prudent decision to pass up the couch. As Elissa pointed out, she could always find a similar couch on sale after she set aside money to pay for it.

YOUR CREDIT FILE

Most of us have no idea what's in our credit file, so it comes as a rude shock when, like Scott, we are denied credit. A credit bureau collects credit information about consumers and sells it to businesses making decisions about granting credit. This system enables creditors to check your record on paying debts to stores and banks and to see if any lawsuits have been filed against you or if you have filed for bankruptcy. Before granting credit, creditors will scrutinize your credit history, income, and expenses, and look for signs of personal stability such as how long you've held your job and have lived in your current home.

By law, whenever you apply for a loan or credit card, you must be notified of the decision within thirty days. You are entitled to a written notice if your application for credit is denied. The notice must state the reasons, although the explanation can be vague. For example, reasons include "unfavorable information in your credit file" or "insufficient income," which doesn't tell you much. Consumers are entitled to review their credit files, however, so you can contact the credit bureau for more information.

To find your credit file, call a local department store and ask the name of the general credit bureau for your area. Then contact the bureau, which will send you a form to fill out. You might be charged a nominal fee of $4 to $10 for this service, but the information must be furnished free if you were turned down for credit within the past thirty days. After the bureau receives your form, it will tell you what's in your file or send you a copy of your credit record. Except in a few states, including California and New York, the law does not require the bureau to make written disclosures about your credit file. However, in practice, most bureaus will give you a written report if you request one.

You can request a reinvestigation if you want to correct an error in your file. If the credit bureau can't verify an item you question, it must be deleted. The reinvestigation may not satisfy you. In that case, write a statement of about one hundred words explaining your side of the dispute, which will be placed in your file. If your file is revised, ask the credit bureau to notify people it recently supplied with data to tell them changes have been made. You can also add a one hundred-word statement to your record explaining the circumstances if you miss payments due to an unusual occurrence such as a sudden loss of income.

Women should be careful about not losing their individual credit ratings when they marry because they are likely to have trouble reestablishing credit on their own. Wives who share joint credit accounts with their husbands should make certain that the account is reported to the credit bureau in both names—for instance, Paul Hunter and Sue Hunter, not Mr. and Mrs. Paul Hunter. Then, as long as the bills are paid promptly, Sue Hunter will be establishing her own good credit history, which is essential should she get divorced or if her husband becomes seriously ill or dies.

If you think a creditor has turned you down unfairly or denied you credit based on your sex or race, contact the federal agency that monitors the creditor. The name and address of the federal agency should be stated on the letter informing you of your rejected credit application.

Scott obtained a computerized printout of his credit file. It stated that one department store account had been delinquent for 120 days, although the current balance on the account was zero. Scott remembered the mixup concerning that bill. It was for $27, and he had overlooked paying it before going to Europe for a semester. When he returned he found several threatening letters from the store and had immediately paid the bill. He thought the problem had been satisfactorily resolved; instead, it was preventing him from obtaining credit.

Scott wrote an explanation and sent it to the credit bureau, attaching a note saying he wanted his explanation included in his file. The credit bureau had an obligation to send his revised credit file to the department store where he had recently applied for a charge account. If Scott applied again, permission to open the charge account would most likely be granted.

CHOOSING A BANK

A bank used to be the place where you opened a checking account for your daily money needs and stashed excess savings in a passbook account (paying 5¼ percent interest). The deregulation of the financial services industry changed all that, blurring the traditional lines between banks, brokerage firms, and insurance companies. Consumers now have a wider selection of financial products and services as companies compete to handle their assets. Choosing where to keep your money is not a simple matter.

But worry no more.

You may wonder whether you need a bank at all. After all, you can keep your savings in a money market mutual fund, which, unlike many banks, won't charge you service fees for looking up your balance or for writing checks. Or you could open a combined assets brokerage account that links your securities investments to a checking account, a line of credit, and a money market fund. But for a novice, neither of these alternatives is as practical as an everyday checking account.

Daily practicality aside, you should establish a relationship with a bank for the sake of your long-term financial needs. At some later stage in life, you will probably want a personal loan or a mortgage for your home or the advice of a banker on a financial transaction.

Banks vary by the products and services they offer, and fees charged to their customers:

- Commercial banks. These "full-service" banks offer checking accounts, savings accounts, mortgages, bank credit cards (Visa and MasterCard), consumer loans, safe deposit boxes, and special checks (for instance, travelers' and cashier's checks).
- Mutual savings banks. Existing primarily in the northeast and Washington state, they used to be limited mostly to savings plans, mortgages, and home improvement loans, but now offer checking accounts and consumer loans, too.
- Savings and loans. They offer many of the same services as commercial banks, but their primary specialty remains mortgage lending.
- Credit unions. If you belong to one through your employer, union, trade association, church, or other organization, you can get the same services other banks provide but often at a lower cost. Credit unions are not operated for profit and are exempt from the federal 5½ percent interest-rate ceiling, so they usually pay a higher interest rate on savings than other institutions. They can be more flexible about making loans, too.

Each type of financial institution offers a range of checking accounts:

- A conventional checking account pays no interest on your balance. You generally can write an unlimited number of checks each month and will be required to maintain a minimum balance or pay a per-check or monthly service fee. If you write many checks, choose a flat service fee; if you write few checks, choose a per-check fee. These accounts are best for people who keep on average $500 or less in the account; if you keep a larger balance, an interest-bearing checking account is a better deal.

- A NOW (Negotiable Order of Withdrawal) account is similar to a regular checking account except it pays you 5¼ percent interest. Service fees and the minimum balance requirement often are higher than for a regular checking account. For example, on average, banks charge $2 to $8 a month and 20 cents to 50 cents per check if your balance slips below a required minimum that ranges from $50 to $2,500, according to a 1984 study by the Consumer Federation of America. You generally have unlimited check-writing privileges.

- A Super NOW account requires a minimum deposit of $2,500 and, if you keep a balance of that amount or more, it pays a higher interest rate—usually about two percentage points higher—than a NOW account. Keep less in your account and you earn only the NOW account rate. Therefore, a Super NOW is advisable only if you can ensure the minimum balance requirement will be met at all times. But even then there are drawbacks to Super NOWs: the service fees charged may be as high as $10 a month, and money market deposit accounts often pay up to one percentage point more in interest. You have unlimited check-writing privileges.

- A money market deposit account requires a minimum deposit of $1,000 to $2,500 and pays you market interest rates. If your account slips below the minimum, though, you won't receive more than the 5¼ NOW account rate for the rest of the month or until the balance reaches the minimum amount required. You can make in-person withdrawals at any time and are allowed to write three checks each month to a third party on the account.

- A sweep account combines a checking and savings account. Generally, your first $1,000 to $2,500 is "swept" into a NOW account that typically pays 5¼ percent interest. Your excess funds are swept into a money market fund that pays you market interest rates. You can write as many checks as you want. These accounts have become less popular since banks began offering the more convenient money market deposit accounts.

- An asset management account is intended to handle all your financial needs. Aimed at the upscale market and slowly growing more popular, these accounts offer a personal banker to attend to your needs, a discount on loans (typically, one-quarter percent lower than other banking customers receive), unlimited checking, a debit card, an automated teller machine card linked to banks around the country, and a discount brokerage service. Other benefits include free attendance at bank-conducted seminars, a travel card, and discounts on travelers' checks. The minimum balance required varies by bank from $10,000 to $20,000. Service fees range from $5 to $12 a month. Your interest rate varies from zero on your checking account to a market rate that floats weekly on your money market account.

Don't keep excess funds lying around in a low-yielding checking account. Keep to a minimum the amount over the balance necessary to cover your daily transactions and needs. The interest rates banks pay on checking accounts are generally less competitive than other investment opportunities.

Consider these factors when you shop for a checking account:

- Convenience. During what hours is the bank open? Evenings? Saturdays? Are there twenty-four-hour cash machines in convenient locations near your home and office? If you travel a lot, ask if the bank belongs to a national network of automated teller machines, enabling you to withdraw funds when you are away from home.

- Service. How many days must you wait to draw on funds you deposit? Will the bank warn you if you are about to overdraw your account? Will you have overdraft privileges, so the bank automatically covers your checks up to a predetermined limit?
- Fees. Penalties for bounced checks for regular checking accounts range from $7 to $20, so ask. Will the bank charge you to look up the balance of your account? What's the penalty if your balance drops below the required minimum? Is the minimum balance requirement computed as an average per month or per quarter or a fixed dollar amount? You are more likely to meet the minimum requirement if it's computed as an average.
- Will shuffling accounts save you money? For example, you might come out ahead by closing your regular checking account and opening an interest-bearing NOW account, as long as you can meet and maintain the higher NOW minimum. The higher the monthly fee you now pay for regular checking, the more you might gain from switching to a NOW account. See if it's worth it to switch based on these factors: the NOW minimum (usually about $1,000), the current monthly checking charges, the monthly amount you're earning on your savings, and the combined monthly amount you'd earn with your savings and a NOW account at 5¼ percent.

SOURCES OF LOANS

As Tom discovered when his car stopped running, sudden emergencies require raising cash in a hurry. Don't wait for a crisis to think about loan sources.

There are two types of loans: unsecured, which means you borrow based on your good name; and secured, which require you to put up collateral or property that the lender collects if you default.

Depending on the loan and amount you want, you may choose from several sources:

Bank Credit Cards

A fast but expensive way to raise cash is through the line of credit extended on your bank credit card. Your bank generally will provide a line of credit equal to the maximum amount you are allowed to charge. If you haven't charged up to your limit, you can ask for the balance of your credit line in cash. You don't need bank authorization. Beware: the annualized interest rate can be 18 percent or higher.

Overdraft Protection

This "revolving" loan connected to your checking account allows you to write checks for more than the amount you have on deposit in your account, up to a predetermined limit. Checks that exceed the balance in the account are considered loans and are subject to interest charges. As with a bank credit card, you can repay a minimum amount each month. You can borrow again, up to your predetermined limit, as soon as you pay off a portion of the debt.

Installment Loans

You borrow a fixed amount from a commercial bank, mutual savings bank, or savings and loan institution and repay it in monthly installments over a specified time period; for instance, two or three years. The terms vary widely. Credit unions also offer these loans, typically with lower interest rates and longer repayment terms than other banks.

Consumer Finance Companies

These private companies may be the easiest source for your first loan since they grant credit more readily than banks. Having a regular source of income may be the only requirement; however, you may need a co-signer. You will pay a higher interest rate for easier credit—20 to 35 percent is not uncommon.

Friends and Relatives

You can borrow from a relative or friend, but it's usually not a good idea. The advantage, of course, is that you won't have to pay interest at all or you can pay a below-market rate. If you do, set it up as a business transaction to avoid misunderstandings and strains on the relationship. After all, you don't want to be reminded of the money you owe your parents every time you eat dinner with them. Draw up a promissory note (you can buy the forms at a stationary store) documenting the amount borrowed, and express interest charges, if any, in percentage points and by the total dollar amount. Record the repayment schedule: monthly, quarterly, or annually. Both the repayment and the original loan should be made by check so there is a record of all transactions.

If you feel uncomfortable asking for help, consider indirect borrowing: have a friend or relative co-sign your loan agreement.

The Loan Agreement

Before you co-sign or sign a loan agreement with anyone, make sure it doesn't include any of the following clauses, which could cause you grief later on:

- An acceleration clause, which allows the lender to demand the entire unpaid balance when you miss an installment.
- A blanket security interest clause, which gives the lender the right to take your valuables if you default on the loan.

- A confession of judgment, which takes away your right to contest the lender's demand for immediate payment in full, even if you have a good reason for not repaying it.
- A co-signer guaranty, which allows the lender to demand a missed payment from your co-signer without warning or trying to collect from you first.
- An attorney's fee clause, which forces a borrower to pay all the legal fees if there's a lawsuit.

To get one of the following secured loans, you must put up collateral. Should you default you will lose the collateral:

Savings Loans

Most savings and loan institutions will allow you to borrow against money invested in a savings account or certificates of deposit. You pay an interest rate one to three percentage points above what you earn on your savings.

Securities Loans

If you borrow money to buy more stocks, you can get a loan from your bank or brokerage house for up to 50 percent of the market value of your stocks. This allows you to raise cash without selling your stocks. If the value of your securities plummets, however, the bank or broker may ask you to put up additional cash. If you don't use the loan to buy more stocks, you can borrow up to 80 percent of the market value of your securities.

Automobile Loans

With this type of loan, you can generally borrow up to 80 percent of the purchase price of your car by pledging it as collateral. However, some banks will lend almost 100 percent of the purchase price. Automobile loans are available from banks, credit unions, and car dealers, so compare rates. You can generally repay the loan in installments over three to five years.

Second Mortgage Loans

You can borrow against the market value of your house minus the amount owed on your mortgage. For a second mortgage a bank will typically lend up to 80 percent of the value of the house, minus the amount you owe on the first mortgage. For example, if you own a $100,000 house and you owe $60,000 on your first mortgage, a bank may give you a second mortgage up to $20,000 (80 percent of the value of the house, minus $60,000, the amount you owe on the first mortgage). Typically, you repay the second mortgage over three to fifteen years. Warning: The interest rate you pay is higher than a normal mortgage rate.

SHOPPING FOR A PERSONAL LOAN

The power of credit can be intoxicating, encouraging people to buy now and worry later. The undisciplined use of credit and other charge cards leads to dangerous levels of debt, especially for people just getting established. Falling into bad habits, such as paying the minimum monthly amount on a charge card rather than the entire month's charges, is easy, and leads to heavy interest costs added to mounting debts. Limit credit card use to convenience: Charge a month's worth of items in stores and restaurants and pay for them by writing one check when you receive the bill. Don't charge more than you can afford when the bill comes due and you won't incur any interest costs.

If you are carrying a high-interest (18 to 25 percent) debt on your bank card, paying it off should be a top priority, even before putting money in a savings account. Don't assume that since your interest costs are deductible (only true if you itemize on your tax return), there's no hurry to pay off the debt. These charges are higher than the yields from most investments, even with the tax deduction for interest.

How much debt is safe? Many financial experts advise limiting your monthly debt payments (not including your mortgage or rent) to 10 to 15 percent of your take-home pay. Many banks use a rule-of-thumb that to qualify for a personal loan, no more than 40 to 50 percent of your net income should go to pay your debts and housing costs. Banks include the carrying cost of the loan you are requesting in the calculation of 40 to 50 percent of your net income. (If your debts hover at dangerously high levels, consult the budgeting chapters for suggestions on controlling your spending.)

Getting a Loan from Your Bank

Applying for a personal loan from a bank can be intimidating. But there's no need to feel as if you are begging for a favor. You're not. A loan is a two-way business transaction: You pay the bank for the use of its funds and the bank makes money by lending funds to you.

For a personal, unsecured loan, a bank will scrutinize your income, assets, and credit history. The minimum requirement is often two years of work experience and two years of residence in the area, preferably in the same home.

Start your loan search at the bank where you keep your checking account or a savings certificate. You will have more leverage at your regular bank than you have at a bank where you are unknown.

If you don't like the terms of the loan offered, don't give up. Next, try a bank where your employer has a relationship. Getting a loan may be easier if your paycheck can be directly deposited to the bank. Then the bank can debit the loan payments right from your account.

Go to the bank interview armed with the information the bank will ask for: a list of your income, assets, debts, and your plan for repaying the debt. Any additional information that can verify your ability to repay the loan will help. For example, ask your employer to write a memo stating that your salary will increase over the next year or two.

Dress and act conservatively, as you would for any business appointment. Disclose any credit problems you have upfront because chances are the bank will find out about them anyway.

If you have a good excuse—for instance, big debts due to an unexpected illness—honesty will enhance your credibility and you might get the loan.

Compare interest rates and other service charges before deciding on a loan. The rates charged by lenders should be translated into the Annual Percentage Rate, or APR, to compare them equally. Compare the total dollar charges for interest, service fees, and late payment or prepayment penalties. Also compare the amount of the monthly payment, when the first payment is due, and how long you have to repay the loan.

Ask for the specific reason if you are turned down. Then, if there's a blot on your credit record, you can straighten it out with the credit bureau before you apply at another bank. Or you could try another bank immediately; banks differ widely in interpreting credit risks.

Tom found an acceptable used car for $4,000. He made a down payment of $800, and needed a loan for $3,200. He was able to raise $1,200 through the credit line on his bank card, leaving a $2,000 deficiency.

Tom's parents would lend him the $2,000 at no interest, but he didn't want to ask them for help. He preferred paying the interest to a bank to hearing his father lament that Tom didn't go to law school like his younger brother.

The only outstanding debt Tom had was a college loan, which he pays back in monthly installments of $40. Tom's first stop was the bank in the same building as his office. His paychecks were directly deposited to his checking account, and the bank looked up his record and saw that he had never overdrawn his account.

The bank was willing to grant him a three-year installment loan. They would debit his loan payments directly from his account, so that as long as he remained employed by the station, there was little risk that he could default. Tom tried two other banks and found little difference in the rates, so he chose his own bank for the sake of convenience and continuity. Within a few days, Tom was driving his new car.

5

INVESTMENTS

SUE AND PAUL WERE DRIVING HOME FROM A COCKTAIL party and discussing their impressions of the guests.

"That guy Bill, the doctor, really annoyed me with his incessant bragging about his stocks," Sue complained.

"He bothered me, too. Probably because we haven't figured out what to do with our $20,000 inheritance. We should be getting the money any day now."

"I know," Sue said. "What are we going to do?"

"We could ask Bill the name of his broker. Then we could bore all our friends," Paul joked.

"My parents would never forgive us if we gambled Grandpa's money on high-flying stocks. Forget it," Sue said.

"I've been meaning to read that information you brought home on mutual funds. I promise I'll do it tomorrow," Paul said.

"That's what you said last weekend and the weekend before. Maybe I should just call Dad for advice," Sue said.

"No, we can't keep asking your father," Paul said. "We have to learn how to handle our own money."

Tom flipped through the business section of the newspaper, gazing at the advertisements and wondering what they meant. His uncle had recently died, leaving him $6,000, which he had put in a passbook savings account. He wanted to withdraw the money and get a better interest rate, but every time he tried to read an article describing bank certificates of deposit or Treasury bills or stock mutual funds, his mind wandered.

He was trying to learn. Last week he invited Richard, the station's business reporter, to lunch to ask his advice about investing. Instead, they spent the hour gossiping.

"It's only $6,000. Why bother to learn all this information for such a meager amount?" he thought. "When I have $20,000 saved, I'll either figure it out or find a stockbroker to deal with it." He walked over to the television set. The football game was about to begin.

After paying his monthly bills, Roy stared at his checking account balance. Almost $3,000, thanks to his moonlighting. What a switch from his days as an intern when a $30 balance made him feel flush.

One thing hadn't changed. He still didn't have any free time. A vacation was out this year, despite the $10,000 he had saved. He wished his money worked as hard as he did, instead of just sitting around in his money market fund earning 8 percent.

"I wouldn't mind playing the stock market with some of this cash," he thought. But he barely had time to keep up with his medical journals, let alone read about investing. A third-year resident couldn't walk out of eye surgery to check his stocks in the newspaper or to call his broker. "I guess this stuff can wait a few years until I'm established in my practice. An 8 percent return, before taxes, is better than nothing," he thought.

INVESTING

No investment will make you rich overnight. But when you're young, fairly affluent, and can afford risk, you have the opportunity to build your assets steadily, assuming you stick to sound financial principles.

How much risk you're willing to take for potential rewards is your most important investment decision. All other investment choices spring from it. A universal rule: The greater the risk you take, the more you stand to make—or lose.

As a beginning investor, restrict your investments to three

categories: money market investments; long-term, fixed-income securities; and stocks. Each has a different ratio of risk to reward.

Sure, there are several other types of investments with exotic names and characteristics; for instance, oil and gas limited partnerships, jojoba bean tax shelters, and real estate syndication deals. These have big drawbacks for novices, however. They tie up your money for too long and are too risky or too difficult to evaluate.

Stick to the basics. Money market investments, long-term fixed-income securities, and stocks offer a wide choice of risk levels, returns, tax protection, and ease of buying and selling. Once your **portfolio** (your total investment holdings) includes the basics and you are comfortable with higher risks, you can graduate to more sophisticated investments.

The best way for young professionals with limited capital to achieve a diversified portfolio is to invest in **mutual funds**, which are companies that pool and invest funds for individuals. There are two types of mutual funds for both stocks and bonds. **Load funds** are bought through sales people and stockbrokers; no-load funds are bought directly through the fund. A no-load fund doesn't charge investors any service fees to buy or sell shares of the fund. Low-load funds charge shareholders either a fee of 1 to 3 percent of their investment when they join the fund or 1 to 3 percent of any shares they redeem.

Load funds typically charge investors a fee of up to 8.5 percent to cover the salesperson's costs and the costs of distributing the fund's shares. For example, if you invested $1,000 in an 8.5 percent load fund, $85 of it would go to the fund's fees and commissions, leaving $915 as the actual amount of your investment.

There is no evidence that load funds outperform no-load funds, so in general buy a no-load fund with a proven track record over many years and market cycles. If you find a load fund with a great performance record, however, don't worry about the sales charge. For example, an 8.5 percent load would be insignificant on a fund that returns 20 percent annually for five years and more than doubles your money.

For now, your investment strategy should consist of two parts. First, decide how to spread your money among these three investments—money market instruments, stocks, and long-term securities. Then, choose the individual investments. Formulating a strategy will prevent you from buying and selling random investments at whim, without considering how each one fits into your overall plan.

Before you allocate your money, you should understand the risks, returns, and the mechanics of each one.

MONEY MARKET INVESTMENTS

Money market investments, in essence, are loans to the government, banks, or corporations that come due in less than one year. They are considered "liquid," which means you may redeem them easily at any time. Because of their short lives you can think of them as cash. You receive a stable rate of return and there is virtually no risk that you will lose your initial investment. The interest rates on all of them are similar.

Common money market investments include:

- **Treasury bills (T-bills).** They have maturities of three months, six months, and one year, and are sold by the U.S. government. T-bills are loans to the government so there is no risk of default. Unless you buy them through a mutual fund (explained below), the minimum amount you can invest is $10,000. The interest you receive on the bill is not taxed by state and local governments. Over the last fifteen years, the interest rate has ranged from 3 to 17 percent. If you must sell a T-bill before it comes due, you usually won't have any problem because there's a ready market of buyers for government bills. You'll have to pay a broker's commission, though, if you sell it early. You can buy T-bills directly through a Federal Reserve bank* or, for a service fee of $15 to $75, through a stockbroker or a bank.

- **Short-term certificates of deposit (CDs).** These bank certificates have terms of one month to one year and are sold by banks and stock brokerage firms. In all but five states they are always federally insured; in those exceptions they can be backed by state associations or private insurance corporations. Your minimum investment is smaller than for Treasury bills, but there are early-withdrawal penalties. The minimum penalty on thirty-one-day to one-year CDs is one month's interest on the amount withdrawn, plus any additional fees levied by the bank. The yields can be higher or lower than on Treasury bills, depending on a bank's need for funds. Shop around for the best rates. Don't put any of your emergency savings cushion in CDs or other investments whose early withdrawal penalties exceed one month's interest.

- **Money market mutual funds.** These funds, issued by investment companies, pool investors' money to buy Treasury bills, certificates of deposit, commercial paper (short-term notes issued by corporations), and other short-term securities. Interest rates fluctuate daily, but follow yields on T-bills and CDs. Unlike bank deposits, the funds are not insured by the federal government, but historically they have been super-safe.

Money can be moved in and out with ease. You can generally open an account with an investment of $250 to

---

*You can buy Treasury bills, notes, and bonds directly from one of the 37 Federal Reserve banks and offices or at the Treasury Building in Washington, D.C., and not pay any service charges. For more information, send for the free booklet, "Buying Treasury Securities at Federal Reserve Banks," Federal Reserve Bank of Richmond, Public Services Department, Box 27622, Richmond, VA 23261.

$500, leave money in as long as you like, or withdraw it anytime without penalty. You can write checks—usually for $250 to $500—on your account and your money keeps earning interest until the check clears.

If your marginal tax bracket is 40 percent or higher, you may prefer a fund that invests only in tax-exempt securities because that interest escapes federal taxation (see Appendix IV for chart on tax-free equivalent yields). Tax-free funds yield about half of what taxable funds yield.

When a money market fund is a member of a mutual fund "family," a group of funds managed by the same company, you can shift money from one fund to another to adapt to changing market conditions. Record-keeping is easy: You will receive periodic account statements stating dividend earnings.

To open an account, ask the investment company that manages the account to send you a prospectus with an application form. You can choose from over 300 money market funds. For a complete, free listing of funds, write to the Investment Company Institute, 1775 K Street, NW, Washington, DC 20006.

- **Bank money market accounts.** These are just like money market mutual funds except they are sponsored by banks, and are backed by the **Federal Deposit Insurance Corporation (FDIC)**, a government agency that insures accounts up to $100,000 at member banks. You can open an account with a minimum deposit of $1,000 to $2,500. Rates fluctuate but can trail money market mutual funds, so you may be sacrificing yield for absolute safety. Because rates vary—sometimes by one percentage point within the same city—shop around. If you plan on keeping more than $5,000 in this account, negotiate with the bank or savings and loan for a higher interest rate. Some institutions pay depositors with big accounts as much as one percentage point more than savers with small accounts.

Recommendation

For most young professionals, money market mutual funds are the best way to invest in money market investments. The funds are convenient to use and allow you to switch money easily to other funds within the same mutual fund family.

Buying individual T-bills and CDs isn't as convenient as using money market accounts because you must keep track of maturity dates and reinvest the proceeds. If you are willing to spend the extra time managing your money, however, T-bills and CDs usually pay slightly higher rates. In addition, the interest on T-bills is exempt from state and local taxes, which can increase your return as much as 10 percent.

LONG-TERM BONDS

Long-term **bonds** are securities issued by federal, state, or local governments or corporations when they want to raise capital. State or local bonds are called **municipal bonds**. Bonds normally sell for $1,000 each in face value (the amount of money printed on the bond's face), which you get back on the date the bonds mature. The term to maturity for long-term bonds is usually between five years and thirty years. Until that date, you receive periodic payments of interest. Usually, you buy new long-term bonds for an amount equal or nearly equal to the face value.

When a bond is sold below face value, it is called selling at a discount. Discount bonds are older bonds whose prices have declined due to rising interest rates. Because interest rates on new bonds are higher than on older bonds, the older bonds must sell for less than their face value to attract buyers. When a bond is selling for a premium, it means its price now exceeds the price you paid for it, which occurs when interest rates fall.

One risk you face with corporate and municipal long-term bonds is that the bond issuer may "default" on the bond or fail to make interest payments. You can, however, minimize your risk by buying only bonds rated A or better by Standard & Poor's

Corporation and Moody's Investors Service Incorporated, the two standard bond rating services. Their reports are available at public libraries. Lower-rated bonds usually pay higher interest rates to compensate for the added risk.

You can invest in long-term securities through:

- **U.S. Government Treasury notes and bonds.** Notes mature in one to five years; bonds mature in five years to thirty years. There's no risk of default because they are backed by the government. You can sell them easily and at any time. You can buy Treasury notes and bonds for a minimum investment of $1,000 directly at a Federal Reserve bank (see footnote on page 88), or through a banker or broker for a service fee of about $25 to $50.

- **Federal agency bonds.** Issued by various agencies such as the Federal National Mortgage Association (Fannie Mae), Government National Mortgage Association (Ginnie Mae), and housing authority bonds, they are backed by the federal government to varying degrees, but not as fully as Treasury notes and bonds. For that reason, interest payments are usually slightly higher than on Treasury notes and bonds. You can buy one for a minimum investment of $5,000 to $10,000 on new bonds, or in $1,000 denominations for older bonds. Only commercial and Federal Reserve banks and stockbrokers sell them. You don't pay a service fee when you buy newly issued bonds, but older bonds carry a fee of about $10 per $1,000.

- **U.S. savings bonds.** These are five- to eleven-year bonds. Interest rates are set at 85 percent of Treasury note yields, with a minimum rate of 7.5 percent. The lowest denomination is a $50 bond that sells for $25 with a ten-year maturity. Interest is exempt from state and local taxes and postponed from federal taxes until you cash in the bond. You buy savings bonds at any bank or through employer-sponsored payroll savings plans. You will pay a substantial penalty for cashing them in early, which makes them best suited to people with long-term savings habits—for example, those who are putting money away for retirement.

- **Bank certificates of deposit (long-term).** They are similar to the certificates of deposit described earlier, but their maturities are longer than one year and early withdrawal penalties are a minimum three months' interest on the amount withdrawn. You may be able to set up a CD on your own terms—for example, eighteen months or twenty-six months. Don't be afraid to haggle with your bank.

- **Municipal bonds.** Issued by state and local governments, their interest is exempt from federal taxes, and usually from state and local taxes where they are issued. Interest rates are lower than on similar taxable investments and therefore these bonds are most attractive to people in high (40 percent and up) marginal tax brackets. You can generally purchase one for $5,000 and buy or sell it easily through a stockbroker. Defaults are rare on top-rated municipals (A or better).

- **Corporate bonds.** These bonds, issued by companies, are riskier than government bonds, but their yields are higher. Your risk can be minimized by sticking to issues with ratings of A or better. They can be bought and sold through a stockbroker at any time. The minimum investment is $1,000, but most brokers trade bonds in blocks of $5,000 or more.

- **Unit trusts.** Brokerage houses assemble these large diversified bond portfolios and sell them in $1,000 units. The interest rate doesn't change because the same bonds remain in the portfolio at all times. Dividends are usually paid monthly, and in some trusts you can automatically reinvest them. The portfolio isn't managed, so you pay no annual management fee. However, sales charges may be as high as 5 percent per $1,000 unit and the trust may include bonds that you wouldn't want to buy as individual securities. You can buy unit trusts consisting of bonds with different terms and objectives.

- **Bond mutual funds.** Like other mutual funds, these bond funds are sponsored by investment companies that pool investors' funds to buy and sell an assortment of bonds. Professionally managed, they are convenient for investors with limited savings who wish to take advantage of long-term bond rates. You can invest with $250 to $500, and add or withdraw money by mail or phone. Funds specialize in U.S. government, corporate, and municipal bonds with different safety ratings and risk levels. For a free, complete listing of mutual bond funds write: Investment Company Institute, 1775 K Street, NW, Washington, DC 20006.

Researching a Bond Investment

Don't buy a bond before checking each of these four factors:

1. Ratings. Not all bonds are equally safe, although those issued by the government are probably the safest. Moody's Investors Services, Incorporated, and Standard & Poor's Corporation publish research reports rating the credit of various bonds, from triple A (the safest) to C or D (lowest quality). Bonds rated A and higher offer the least risk. Riskier bonds should offer higher interest rates.
2. Value. You will encounter three important calculations of interest rates on each bond. Coupon rate is the interest payment as a percent of the bond's face value. Current yield is the interest payment as a percent of the bond's current price. Yield to maturity is the interest rate based on the bond's current price plus the gain or loss when the bond matures.

    To determine the bond value for bonds with maturities longer than ten years, current yield is usually all you need to look at. Current yields tell you what your interest payments will be and are listed in the financial sections of many newspapers. On bonds maturing in less than ten years, examine both the annual interest payments plus the amount of principal you'll get back at maturity. The current yield will indicate your annual income on the bond; yield to maturity will indicate annual payments and payment at maturity. (This calculation is explained in detail in Appendix I.)

3. Maturities. Bonds are issued with set **maturity** dates. As long as you wait until maturity to redeem the bond, you are guaranteed the return of your principal. But if you need to sell it sooner, you may lose money on it. To minimize this risk, buy bonds with maturities on or before the date when you anticipate needing the money. In general, bonds with longer maturities should pay higher interest rates because there is greater risk that you can lose some of your principal.

4. Callable. If a bond is callable, it means the issuer may redeem it at a stated price before its date of maturity, and after a predetermined number of years. Make sure to check when a bond is callable before you buy it.

Recommendation

For young professionals, the best way to invest in long-term bonds is through municipal bond funds. These mutual funds provide a high rate of tax-free return, as well as convenience and professional management. Look for a fund whose portfolio consists mostly of highly rated (A or better) bonds. To minimize the risk of losing your principal, select a bond fund with maturities that are generally less than twenty years.

One caveat: If you're not in a high tax bracket (40 percent or higher) then corporate bond funds, which are not tax-exempt, are preferable because they pay a higher rate of return.

STOCKS

Stocks are shares of ownership in a company. As part owner of a profitable company, you may periodically receive **divi-**

dends (payments distributed to shareholders). The value of your shares of stock may increase or decrease as investors' perceptions of the company's fortunes change. Any change in the value of a stock is called a **capital gain** or **capital loss**.

There are no guarantees that the money you invest in stocks will grow. You could even lose your entire investment. Yet, people continue to risk their money in the stock market because it promises greater potential returns than other investments.

Stock prices fluctuate daily and are sensitive to interest rates, the general state of the economy, and business conditions.

Hundreds of theories attempt to predict stock prices, based on everything from which team wins the Super Bowl to calculations of a company's future earnings. In truth, nobody really knows what drives stock prices.

Professional stock analysts rely on two formulas to help them judge if a stock is selling at a fair price:

1. **Yield.** This is the amount of dividends per share paid out in the last year divided by the stock price. If you bought a stock for $100 a share and received annual dividends of $10 per share, the stock would yield 10 percent.
2. **Price/earnings (P/E) ratio.** This is the price of a share of stock divided by the company's most recent twelve months' earnings per share. Earnings are company profits after all expenses and taxes have been paid, but before dividends are paid out to shareholders. A stock selling for $50 per share that earned $5 over the last twelve months has a P/E ratio of 10. You can find the P/E ratio listed in *The Wall Street Journal* and *USA Today.* A stock with a high P/E generally indicates that the company's earnings are expected to grow rapidly. A low P/E indicates that the company is in a mature industry with stable earnings.

Stocks can be classified as either growth or income stocks or a combination of both. Income stocks are well-established companies that pay steady dividends with high yields of 5 to 10 percent. Growth stocks are companies in new or emerging industries or markets that pay little or no dividends; instead, the company reinvests all profits in expansion of the business. Since earnings of growth companies are expected to increase substantially, they often sell at high P/E ratios.

Investors buy growth stocks expecting them to appreciate considerably. For example, an investor who paid $11 a share for Apple Computer, Incorporated, in 1982 could have sold it for $63 a share in early 1983. It dropped to $20 a share in late 1983, illustrating the volatility of growth stocks.

Buying growth stocks has tax advantages. You're betting that most of your return will come as **appreciation** on the stock price (capital gain) when you sell the stock at a profit. Only 40 percent of a long-term capital gain is taxable.

No matter how good a stock looks, don't invest more than 5 percent of your money in any individual stock (or bond). Otherwise, your risk is too high that one company's poor performance will drag down the value of your portfolio. **Diversification** of your holdings reduces risk.

How to Pick Your Own Stocks

It takes considerable knowledge and effort to pick your own stocks. If you don't want to devote your free time to interpreting financial reports, hire a stockbroker to provide you with research on companies and investment advice.

You pay a **broker** through commissions on stocks, bonds, and other investments. Commissions vary depending on the price of the stock and the amount of shares you buy. As a novice, use a full-service broker unless you want to commit a great deal of time and effort to researching and selecting your own stocks. If you prefer to do the leg work yourself, use a discount broker. A discount broker will only execute your buy and sell orders, not provide advice or research reports. The commissions paid to discount brokers are up to 70 percent lower than those paid to full-service brokers. (See Chapter 7, Financial Advisers.)

Even if you don't want to pick your own stocks, if you know how, you can check your broker's recommendations. Professional analysts evaluate a company based on either a **fundamental** or **technical analysis**. Fundamentalists look at factors such as a company's sales, assets, rising or falling earnings, potential markets, products, and management. Fundamental stock analysts generally look for affirmative answers to these questions:

- Is the price/earnings ratio equal to or lower than that of similar companies in the same industry? This is the most important question, since it determines whether a stock is overpriced. The biggest mistake novice investors make is investing in good companies that are already overpriced relative to their earnings.
- Are earnings expected to increase? If earnings rise, so should the stock price.
- Does the company have new products that are expected to increase earnings in the next few years?
- Are the company's products or services competitive with those of other companies?
- Does the company have strong management?

Technicians study only price patterns of the stock and technical signs in the market, such as the number of shares traded daily. There are large followings of investors in both camps, so stay attuned to both by further reading of books, magazines, newspapers, and newsletters (see bibliography).

For more detailed stock research and analysis, start with the two industry bibles, "The Value Line Investment Survey" and Standard & Poor's "The Outlook," both available at public libraries. These fact sheets on companies tell you the earnings of each, the number of shares outstanding, how much debt the company has, and other essentials. "Value Line" covers 1,700 stocks, divided by industry, and ranks stocks by their safety and timeliness. "The Outlook" recommends different portfolios for investors, with five to ten stocks in each.

Read other publications for investment ideas and advice. Start with your local newspaper's business section, which features stories on local and regional companies. For example, do you go to a department store or restaurant that is usually jammed? Investigate the individual company or chain to which it belongs.

National publications geared to individual investors and loaded with useful information are *Forbes,* the Money section of *USA Today,* and *Money* magazine, all of which contain many stories geared to young professionals. For general business information read *The Wall Street Journal* and watch "Wall Street Week in Review" on PBS.

Stock Mutual Funds

Another alternative to picking your own stocks is to buy them through a stock mutual fund. Like bond mutual funds, these funds pool investors' money to buy and sell a wide selection of stocks. Mutual funds invest in a particular type of stocks, such as growth or income, or according to a particular investment philosophy or theory. For example, a contrarian fund buys stocks with low price-earning ratios currently out of vogue with Wall Street trends. You can usually figure out the fund's investment objectives by its name, but before you buy anything, read the prospectus and the list of stocks it invests in.

Stock mutual funds are the best alternative for small investors. You can buy shares with a small initial investment (usually $250 to $500) and receive professional management from a full-time fund manager. Still, there are no guarantees that your fund will be a winner, even if it's been a top performer. The fund manager invests in a wide variety of stocks, reducing your risk should any one stock or group of stocks go down in value.

You can withdraw funds easily by mail (for $250 or more) or move money within the same mutual fund family. You will receive periodic financial statements from the fund, thus reducing your record-keeping. These services are paid for through a small management fee—typically, one-half percent of the fund's annual return, regardless of whether the fund is load or no-load.

Recommendation

For young professionals with less than $20,000 who want to invest in the stock market, mutual funds offer the best opportunities. To achieve a diversified portfolio with less than $20,000, the amount you could invest in any individual stock would be small, and many brokers wouldn't pay adequate attention to your account. A growth mutual fund is the most advantageous because of its favorable tax treatment.

If you have more than $20,000 to invest, use a stockbroker, as you're probably too busy to research and choose your own stocks. Therefore, finding a good stockbroker is critical (see Chapter 7, Financial Advisers).

A HISTORICAL LOOK AT RISK VERSUS RETURNS

The table on page 100 compares the returns on the three investment categories of money market instruments, long-term securities, and stocks during the last thirty years. Money market instruments are represented by ninety-day Treasury bills; long-term securities are represented by the Dow Jones 20 Bond Average, an index of major corporate bonds used to indicate the direction of the bond market; and stocks are represented by Standard & Poor's composite index of 500 stocks.

The first column, "Index," shows how much money you'd have if you had invested $100 in 1952. The "Annual Percentage Change" column shows the percentage change in the value of your investment each year.

- Returns on money market instruments varied from less than 1 percent in 1954 to 14 percent in 1981. There is no risk of losing your principal with short-term instruments so the returns are never negative.
- Returns on long-term securities varied from a high of 38.5 percent in 1982 to a low of minus 5.5 percent in 1956. Bond returns are often higher than short-term money market in-

Table 5:1—Total Return—Price Plus Income Reinvested

Year	Money Market Instruments Index	Annual % Change	Long-Term Securities Index	Annual % Change	Stocks Index	Annual % Change
1952	100.0		100.0		100.0	
1953	102.0	1.95%	101.8	1.84%	98.1	−1.91%
1954	102.9	0.95%	109.2	7.27%	154.1	57.06%
1955	104.7	1.75%	109.8	0.47%	207.9	34.96%
1956	107.5	2.68%	103.8	−5.48%	222.5	7.02%
1957	111.1	3.29%	105.5	1.73%	197.9	−11.08%
1958	113.1	1.85%	108.1	2.40%	281.7	42.33%
1959	117.0	3.44%	105.5	−2.35%	317.3	12.64%
1960	120.5	2.97%	115.7	9.60%	312.5	−1.50%
1961	123.4	2.39%	119.3	3.16%	395.9	26.69%
1962	126.8	2.80%	130.4	9.25%	356.8	−9.87%
1963	130.9	3.18%	136.8	4.97%	441.7	23.79%
1964	135.5	3.59%	144.5	5.56%	513.8	16.32%
1965	141.0	3.99%	145.9	1.02%	577.8	12.44%
1966	147.9	4.94%	141.7	−2.87%	519.9	−10.01%
1967	154.4	4.38%	137.1	−3.25%	644.1	23.89%
1968	162.8	5.42%	143.3	4.47%	715.3	11.04%
1969	173.8	6.80%	139.8	−2.41%	655.1	−8.41%
1970	185.2	6.54%	163.5	16.92%	680.7	3.90%
1971	193.3	4.38%	183.0	11.95%	777.5	14.22%
1972	201.3	4.11%	198.3	8.37%	924.9	18.97%
1973	215.7	7.15%	205.6	3.64%	789.3	−14.67%
1974	233.0	8.03%	203.8	−0.84%	581.3	−26.35%
1975	246.8	5.93%	233.4	14.52%	796.8	37.08%
1976	259.3	5.06%	286.7	22.83%	986.7	23.83%
1977	273.1	5.33%	302.6	5.54%	915.7	−7.19%
1978	293.1	7.34%	305.2	0.86%	975.4	6.53%
1979	323.5	10.35%	289.3	−5.20%	1155.5	18.45%
1980	361.4	11.74%	279.3	−3.47%	1530.3	32.44%
1981	412.5	14.13%	282.6	1.20%	1454.9	−4.93%
1982	457.2	10.84%	391.3	38.47%	1767.8	21.50%
1983	497.51	8.82%	425.3	8.68%	2164.7	22.46%

(Source: Wright Investor's Service, Bridgeport, Conn.)

vestments, but losses of up to 5 percent in one year do occur. However, once in a while—for example, in the late 1970s—losses reached over 5 percent, primarily because of an unexpected surge in interest rates. When interest rates go up, bond prices historically have fallen, and when interest rates decline, bond prices have risen.

- Returns on stocks have been as high as 57 percent in 1954 and as low as minus 26 percent in 1974. Most of the time, returns were considerably higher than on money market investments and long-term securities. But losses of 10 to 20 percent in one year do occur.

Therefore, the smartest investment strategy is to divide your money among these categories according to your own risk tolerance levels. Stocks clearly are high-risk/high-return investments, something novice investors may lose sight of during boom or bust periods. Money market investments are the only investments that ensure positive returns, although not nearly so high as stocks. Long-term bonds usually have higher returns than money market investments, but there's a chance your capital will erode.

Recommendation

Allocate your funds so that you have at least three to six months' net salary readily available in safe money market investments. Many people prefer to keep at least one-third of their savings in money market investments. More conservative investors may keep at least one-half of their money there.

The portion of your savings invested in long-term securities should be money you want to protect from a major loss. Still, you should be willing to take a little more risk for a higher income than on money market investments.

Your investment in stocks should be the portion of your savings you are willing to risk for a higher return than on money market investments and bonds. Income stocks are safer than growth stocks, but their potential return is lower. There is little chance you would ever lose more than 20 percent of your total investment in one year, but in eleven out of the thirty years shown in the table, returns exceeded 20 percent.

How you divide your money among the three investments depends on your risk tolerance. The more you invest in stocks and bonds, the higher potential you have for loss and/or gain. For example, an aggressive investor will put about one-third of his savings in each type of investment. A moderate investor would put about half his savings in money market funds and half in stocks and bonds. A conservative investor would put two-thirds of his money in money market funds and one-third in bonds.

The examples that follow illustrate these alternatives.

Sue and Paul have $30,000 to invest: $6,000 in a bank passbook savings account yielding 5¼ percent; $4,000 in a taxable money market fund yielding 8 percent, and a $20,000 inheritance. Their best course is to split the $30,000 among three funds in a no-load mutual fund family.

The reason: They can move their money in and out of the various funds as market conditions change. Most of the time, however, Sue and Paul do not have to do anything—and that suits them fine.

Here is how they divided their money:

- $10,000 in a money market fund that invests only in tax-exempt securities. The money is readily available and the principal is safe. They are in a 45 percent marginal tax bracket (filing jointly) so the 6 percent yield is equivalent to a 10.9 percent yield in a taxable fund.
- $10,000 in a long-term municipal bond fund. The interest rate is 9.5 percent tax-free, which is the equivalent of 17.3 percent in a taxable investment for those in their tax bracket (see chart in Appendix IV, page 191, comparing tax-free

equivalent yields). The risk is that if interest rates rise they'll lose some principal. But they expect their overall return to exceed what they would earn in a money market fund.

- $10,000 in a high-growth stock mutual fund, of which $4,000 is invested in two Individual Retirement Accounts. This allows them to share in any stock market gains. For now they are comfortable with investing one-third of their savings at some risk.

Tom is right about one thing: $6,000 is not a large enough sum to split into sophisticated investments. But he can do much better than a 5¼ percent yield—without even leaving his bank.

He should invest $1,500 in a six-month certificate of deposit. He doesn't anticipate needing that cash soon, and the guaranteed interest rate is 10 percent, almost double the rate of his passbook account. While at the bank, he should open a bank money market account with the remaining $4,500. The current yield is 8 percent and he can keeping adding to it. Once he has accumulated more—perhaps another $5,000—he should consider moving his funds into a no-load mutual fund family. That will give him the flexibility of switching to various funds as market conditions change.

When he has accumulated savings beyond $6,000, he should start an Individual Retirement Account (discussed in Chapter 9, Retirement).

Roy enjoys a psychological boost when he looks at his $3,000 checking account balance, but that's a poor reason to keep a large sum in an account earning no interest. He should withdraw $2,000 of it, leaving $1,000 to meet his monthly bills.

Roy should also withdraw half of the $10,000 in his money market fund, leaving himself $5,000 readily available for emergencies. His tax bill is not high enough yet to merit investing in a tax-exempt fund.

Because he is willing to take high risks for potentially high returns, he should invest the $7,000 he has ($2,000 from his checking account, $5,000 from his money market fund) in an aggressive growth stock mutual fund. He should put $2,000 of that $7,000 in an IRA (which will be discussed in greater detail in Chapter 9).

He can afford the risk. Should he lose his confidence in the stock market, he can withdraw part of the money and place it in the money market fund. To make it easy to move money around, the money market fund and the stock fund should belong to the same no-load family. Roy should pick the fund family based on the performance of its growth stock fund over the last ten to fifteen years, not its money market fund performance, which doesn't vary as much. However, there are plenty of no-load funds that have good performance records for several types of funds (see Appendix II for best performing mutual funds of 1983).

6

REAL ESTATE

"LOOK, PAUL, THERE'S A 'FOR SALE' SIGN," SUE SAID AS they drove by a big yellow house. "Let's ring the doorbell and take a look."

"If we go now, we'll be late for dinner. Anyway, this doesn't look like the greatest neighborhood."

"It never hurts to look. Then we'll get a better feel for prices," Sue answered. "We really don't have time to stop now, so I'll copy down the phone number and call tomorrow."

"Don't you think we would be better off calling a real estate agent? We've been looking for three weeks and we haven't found anything."

"We've barely looked at all. There will be plenty of time to bring in an agent," Sue said. "I don't want to be pressured by a hard sell until we have a better idea what's available."

"Okay. But I think we're wasting time."

Rachel knew it would happen eventually. Her apartment building was being converted into condominiums. She had to buy her unit or vacate it.

She wouldn't want to live there forever, but buying made sense. The neighborhood was up and coming, she had a convenient commute to her office, and with the discount given to tenants, the unit was selling for a good price. If she put a little money into fixing up the place—painting it, sanding the floors, building kitchen cabinets—she could probably sell it in a few years for a nice profit, especially if the neighborhood continued to improve.

There was just one problem: money for a down payment. Her parents would probably lend her money, but she hated to ask them with her brother and sister in expensive colleges.

"We're so sorry you're moving," Ellen told David. "We'll really miss you."

"I'll miss you guys, too. But you know teaching jobs in comparative literature are scarce. This one could lead to a tenured position, even if it is in College Park, Maryland."

"At least you'll be near Washington. If Scott ever gets a job it'll probably be in South Dakota. What are you doing with your apartment?"

"I haven't decided yet. Do you want it? It's bigger than yours and closer to the subway. I think the rent is about the same."

"We'd love your apartment, but it's impossible," Ellen said. "We just signed a lease for another year. Too bad. Your apartment is much nicer."

"Maybe there's a way to break the lease," Scott said. "David, don't offer the apartment to anyone else for two days. I'll call my cousin, the real estate lawyer. Maybe we can find a loophole."

RENTING VERSUS BUYING

One of the most important financial decisions you face is whether to buy or rent a home. The answer is not clear-cut like it was during the 1970s, when owning a home was considered the best of all investments. In those days of single-digit **mortgage** rates and 10 percent annual appreciation in home prices, young professionals didn't question the conventional wisdom that home ownership was better than renting. It was. All over the country, condominium and cooperative apartments and townhouses were built or converted for those who couldn't afford or didn't want to maintain single-family houses.

But these days, owning versus renting is a closer call. The

1980s brought rising mortgage rates, a glut of unsold homes, high closing costs, and housing appreciation rates under 5 percent a year. Home ownership will remain more expensive because interest rates will be higher relative to inflation and prices are starting at a steeper level.

So should you buy or rent?

Several factors—some financial, some not—may make renting more desirable than owning, at least for the short term (one to three years). For instance, a housing surplus in some cities means you can rent an apartment or townhouse in a good location for less than it would cost to buy it.

Maybe you're planning to change jobs and move to another city in a year or two. In that case, you don't want to buy anything because property generally appreciates over a long period (at least three to five years). **Closing costs** when you buy and brokerage fees when you sell could exceed any profits from price appreciation.

Another advantage renters have is that they can try different neighborhoods until they find the area in which they'd like to settle. As a renter, you can spend your free time on pursuits other than maintaining, fixing, and improving your home. You won't be hit with unexpected repair costs. Owners often pay more than renters for repairs and utility bills, and renters don't pay any real estate taxes.

Your tax bracket is another consideration (see Chapter 2, Taxes, for how to figure it). The higher it is, the more you save from each dollar of deductible expenses provided by home ownership. The lower your tax bracket, the less incentive you have to buy. Cash flow is another factor. Renting for a few years could enable you to accumulate more savings and buy a better house later.

On the other hand, tax laws are structured to make home ownership more profitable than renting. Home owners can deduct real estate taxes and mortgage interest payments from federal income taxes; renters don't have these deductions.

A home is a leveraged investment. By putting down a little,

you can buy a lot. For example, if you buy a $100,000 house with $10,000 down and it appreciates only 10 percent, you've doubled your investment. Owning allows you to control and plan your future while a renter is at the mercy of landlords. With a fixed-rate, thirty-year mortgage, you know what your mortgage payments will be in ten, twenty, and thirty years. No one can predict rents.

Keeping these points in mind, let's take a closer look at the decision to rent or buy.

First, you must compare what your monthly costs will be in each case. For renting:

- Rental payment. Estimate your monthly rent, based on prevailing rentals in your area. Your calculations should allow for a 5 to 10 percent rent increase each year.
- Utilities. Estimate heat and electricity expenses, based on information provided by landlords and former tenants. Costs vary considerably by building. Get average yearly costs based on twelve months, not one month, because these costs change throughout the year according to outside temperatures.

For buying:

- Monthly mortgage payment. Find out the price range in the area where you would buy by talking to real estate agents and reading classified advertisements.

  To find out the prevailing interest rates, inquire at banks, read newspaper advertisements, and ask people who recently took out mortgages. What are the down payment requirements? A 10 to 20 percent down payment is typical.

  The following chart will help you figure your monthly mortgage payments for different mortgage rates and house costs. The chart is based on a **conventional mortgage** of

Table 6:1—Monthly Mortgage Payments

he mortgage amount, which is purchase price minus down payment, expressed per
ousand.)

	25	50	75	100	125	150	175	200
terest Rate								
8	$183	367	550	734	917	1101	1284	1468
10	219	439	658	878	1097	1316	1536	1755
12	257	514	772	1029	1286	1543	1800	2057
14	296	592	889	1185	1481	1777	2074	2370
16	336	672	1009	1345	1681	2017	2353	2690
18	377	754	1130	1507	1884	2261	2637	3014

thirty years at a fixed rate. For alternative mortgage terms
the results would be slightly different.

- Utilities. Estimate these costs based on the experiences of
previous owners of the unit. If you are considering moving
to a new development, contact local utility offices and ask for
an estimate based on the age and square footage of the unit.
- Real estate taxes. These tax rates vary by locality and can be
obtained from local tax authorities or real estate agents.
These taxes can be considerable and shouldn't be overlooked when calculating your monthly costs. Real estate tax
rates are often quoted in terms of dollars per thousand dollars of house valuation. For instance, if the value of the
house is $80,000 and the tax rate is $20 per thousand, then
the annual real estate tax is $1,600 (80 times 20). In many
areas, for the purpose of real estate taxes, "value" is "as-
sessed value" rather than "actual value." Compute the
monthly real estate tax by dividing the yearly real estate tax
by twelve.
- Maintenance costs. The monthly condo and co-op fees are
the maintenance costs. For houses, the costs will vary considerably depending on its condition and age. Approximate the
costs of major repairs (painting, new floors, roofing, heating
equipment) needed over the next five years to determine an
average expenditure per month.

• Tax savings. Your payments of interest on your mortgage plus your real estate tax payments are deductible from your federal income tax. These savings, in a sense, reduce the actual monthly costs of home ownership. To calculate this savings, take your monthly expenditures for the mortgage payment interest (which in the first five years is almost all of the mortgage payment) plus your real estate taxes and multiply this sum by your marginal tax rate (see Chapter 2, page 25). For instance, if your monthly mortgage payment is $700, your real estate taxes are $150, and your tax rate is 33 percent, this year's monthly tax savings is $281: $700 plus $150, times .33, equals $281.

Now compare the monthly costs for renting versus buying by adding the items pertaining to each.

Rent		**Buy**	
Rent	$____	Mortgage	$____
plus Utilities	____	plus Utilities	____
		plus Real Estate Tax	____
		plus Maintenance	____
		Total Cost	$____
		minus Tax Savings	____
Net cost	$____	Net cost	$____

For example, Tom rents a one-bedroom apartment in a building with a swimming pool and underground parking for $600 a month, plus $28 a month in utilities. He is thinking of buying the unit for $85,000. He can make a $10,000 down payment, which leaves $75,000, on which he can get a 12 percent, fixed-rate, thirty-year mortgage. Real estate taxes will be $100 a month and maintenance costs will be $100 a month. As shown in the following table, Tom calculates that buying will cost him $84 more per month than renting.

Tom's Monthly Costs: Renting Versus Buying

Rent		Buy	
Rent	$600	Mortgage	$772
plus Utilities	28	plus Utilities	28
		plus Real Estate Tax	100
		plus Maintenance	100
		Total Cost	$1,000
		minus Tax Savings	288
Net cost	$628	Net cost	712

While Tom figures that buying will cost him $84 per month more than renting, he must, of course, consider more than his monthly costs. His down payment was $10,000. And closing costs, for sale-related expenses such as legal fees and registration fees, generally amount to 3 to 5 percent of house costs, or $2,400 in this case. Thus, Tom's initial outlay is $12,400.

Tom's Initial Costs and Final Costs in Buying
(Assuming He'll Keep Property Five Years)

Initial Costs		Final Costs (assumes 5 to 8 percent annual appreciation)	
Down Payment	$10,000	Sale	$108,000 to $125,000
plus Closing Costs	2,400	minus Commission	6,000
		minus Mortgage	73,000
Total	$12,400	Net	$ 29,000 to $ 46,000

Whether buying is ultimately profitable for Tom depends on the price he can get for his unit in five years. Tom believes appreciation will be 5 to 8 percent a year since the unit is in a good building in a desirable neighborhood. If so, the selling price would be $108,000 to $125,000. He would have to pay commissions to a real estate agent when he sells the unit. The commission is typically 6 percent of the house price. And he would have to pay off his mortgage. Despite five years of payments, the principal outstanding is just $2,000 less than the initial $75,000. (This is difficult to calculate, but you can generally assume that after five years, on a thirty-year mortgage, you have made only a tiny dent in your mortgage principal.)

Thus, after five years Tom will receive a $29,000 to $46,000 return on his initial investment of $12,400. He also made five years of extra monthly payments of $84 a month (about $5,000). Still, his return is pretty good, even considering the interest Tom could have earned in alternative ways on the invested money.

Tom should buy the unit because his potential for a large profit seems good. If Tom were planning to keep the unit for a year, however, he would be better off renting because the appreciation is unlikely to be sufficient.

This example illustrates points that generally apply to the decision to rent or buy. You should buy if:

- Your monthly payments on a home will be nearly the same or a little higher than renting.
- You expect the home to appreciate.
- You plan to own the home for at least two years.
- You are ready to assume the added responsibilities of home ownership.

Of course, you can usually make money buying property if you're willing to take steps to ensure good appreciation. For instance, you could buy an inexpensive house or apartment, fix it up, and sell it a few years later. You wouldn't necessarily have to move to the place you bought; you could rent it to tenants and still achieve most of the benefits of home ownership discussed here.

BUYING PROPERTY

Deciding to buy a home is often easier than choosing the type of home to buy: a cooperative or condominium apartment, a townhouse, a planned-unit development, or a detached single-family house. Condos, co-ops, and townhouses are good for people who don't want the hassles of home ownership; there are no lawns to mow or roofs to repair. They are generally cheaper than single-family homes of equivalent size and location. The city you live in may determine your choices: it's hard to find a co-op outside of New York City, Chicago, Miami, San Francisco, or a few other places. The legal structure and investment implications differ for each form of home ownership.

Cooperatives

In a co-op, instead of owning an apartment you own shares of stock in a corporation which owns an apartment building, entitling you to live in one of the units. Co-op owners have voting rights in the corporation that owns the building. In some co-ops, each unit is allocated one vote; in others, votes are allocated according to the size of the unit.

Buying a co-op often requires a larger down payment than buying a condo or a house. Financial institutions are stricter about granting credit to co-op buyers because an owner is liable for all debts of the building. This "joint liability" means that if the building is foreclosed, all residents will lose the leases on their individual units. And if one neighbor defaults on his payments, the others must cover his portion of the monthly fees.

In addition to the interest payments on the sum you borrowed to buy your co-op, all residents pay a monthly operating fee to maintain the building, determined by the number of shares allocated each unit. The governing body of the building is the Board of Directors, which must approve the resale or sublet of any unit. Living closely with neighbors and abiding by the rules of the corporation is crucial in a co-op, as it is in a condominium building.

Because your apartment is not a separate property entity, it's harder to get financing for a co-op than for a condo. But there has been some movement to liberalize co-op lending laws, which should make obtaining co-op financing easier. You finance a co-op through a personal loan secured only by your credit rating, not by the value of your property.

Condominiums

You own an apartment in a building, or a freestanding garden apartment, as well as a share in common areas such as land, lobbies, elevators, parking lots, hallways, and swimming pools.

As a condo owner you own the deed to your apartment and pay real estate taxes. Your mortgage loan is secured by your property and you have the same financing options as owners of single-family houses.

Unlike co-op owners, who have a Board of Directors to vote on prospective owners and tenants, condo owners generally (it varies by building) have more freedom to sublet or resell their unit. For these reasons, except in cities where co-ops are more common, it is easier to finance and mortgage a condo.

A condo (or townhouse) can give you amenities you might not be able to afford as a homeowner. These extras have a price. You and the other owners pay dues to a service corporation, usually called the homeowner's association, to maintain and repair the common areas of the building.

The drawbacks to condominium living are: You must abide by the rules and regulations of the homeowner's association. It is not uncommon for associations to have lists of rules on such things as keeping pets or decorating your front door. You can't control future increases in maintenance fees and assessments, which can increase steeply year to year if major repairs are needed.

Before you buy a condo (or co-op) in a converted apartment building, investigate the age and condition of the building and common systems such as heating and wiring. You can hire a contractor to do a professional inspection for about $100 to $300. How much has been set aside in a reserve fund for capital improvements and unexpected repairs to the building? If the amount isn't much, you may be hit with steep maintenance fees. This should not be a concern in a new building, which probably has separate metered heating and cooling systems for each unit. Ask to see copies of past minutes of the homeowner's association meetings. There you are likely to find frank discussions about the problems of the building.

Townhouses

These are row houses connected by common walls with separate entrances for each unit. Amenities such as pools, saunas, tennis courts, and exercise rooms are often included. The legal structure can be set up as a condominium or as a planned-unit development.

Planned Unit Development (PUD)

You own your dwelling as well as the ground underneath it, and often a yard. Unlike condos and co-ops, you may be responsible for outside maintenance. The grounds of a PUD are supervised and owned by a nonprofit association, of which you are a member. PUDs offer the same ownership advantages as a condominium, but you have more flexibility and privacy.

Single-family houses

As wide a range of financing options are available for single-family houses as there are for condominiums. You may be able to assume the mortgage of the previous owners at below-market rates. Many states offer loans for first-time home buyers at below market rates, and if you buy a newly built house the builder may offer financing arranged through a local lender.

You have more freedom to renovate and decorate than in a condo or co-op because houses can go up or out, but you can't expand beyond the exterior unit walls of a condo or co-op. You are free to sell or rent your house without consulting anyone. Of course, as sole owner, you are responsible for maintenance, so be prepared for surprises, especially in an old house.

Historically, single-family houses have appreciated faster than condos and co-ops, probably because it's the form of ownership least restricted by rules and regulations. The median price of a single-family home in the resale market more than tripled between 1968 and 1981, from $20,000 to $62,000. But it may not do so again.

WORKING WITH A REAL ESTATE BROKER

When You Are the Buyer

Once you have decided on the type of home you want and chosen the location, you'll probably need help finding the best property. At that point, call a real estate agent or broker. Once you are close to making an offer on a particular property, you will need to consult a lawyer.

But before you call any real estate agents, do a comparative study of house prices in neighborhoods you like. Then you will be able to spot a good buy when you see one and you won't be easily swayed by the agent. Go to open houses every Sunday in various neighborhoods to get a sense of what an extra bedroom, a larger yard, or a renovated kitchen is worth. Study the classified ads in local newspapers. This will tell you which real estate brokers are active in which neighborhoods and give you a general sense of prices. Keep in mind that advertisements can be deceiving. What one seller calls a five-bedroom house could mean that the living room and dining room were converted into bedrooms. To get a true sense of what's available, you must visit the houses and see for yourself.

Then, you can check the recorded prices of specific houses on specific streets at your city or county clerk's office. In some communities, these records are filed at the public library as well. But a quicker method is to ask your broker for a computer printout of all the homes sold in a particular neighborhood during a given time period. Again, this is not an absolute index of prices because the records will tell you, for example, that House A and House B, identical houses on the same street, sold for $125,000 each. The records won't tell you that the owner of House A has agreed to include the washer and dryer and to fix the leaky roof. You will, however, get a general sense of prices.

As a first-time buyer, be aware that your broker has an economic incentive (a bigger commission) to show you only homes listed by his or her agency. Don't allow that! A good broker will take you to homes listed by other agencies and split the commission.

A broker should be able to ferret out how many offers—if any —have been made on a particular property. That's important because you can usually get a better deal if the house is vacant and the owner has been losing money. Don't be afraid to make a low offer. You can always raise it. The owners may be eager to sell, the house may be overpriced, or it may be the only offer they get. Don't be influenced by agents and sellers trying to pressure you into buying. Exercise your right to walk away from any deal that you don't like, an option often overlooked by people caught up in the frenzy of buying a home.

When you are buying a house, you don't pay the agent's commission—the seller does. That has important implications:

- Unless you buy something, the agent doesn't collect a commission for the services or time he or she has invested in showing you properties. Therefore, the agent has an economic incentive to encourage you to buy a property he or she has shown.
- The higher the price of the property you buy, the higher commission the agent earns, which means the agent has no economic incentive to sell you the lowest-priced property.

- The agent's first loyalty is to the seller of the house, not to you, even though you and the agent may have spent time together and developed a friendly relationship. The personal relationship between purchaser and agent further clouds the bargaining process.

Buyers who are unhappy with this system are turning to an alternative called "buyer's brokerage." Buyers hire and pay their own agent to represent their interests, so as a purchaser you have access to the same skills, services, and training a seller does. The advantages of a buyer's broker:

- The broker is employed and paid by the buyer so he or she is obligated to find you the best possible price and terms.
- The broker can help you buy properties sold outside the brokerage system; for example, homes offered by self-sellers.
- When you are negotiating for a property, because one broker clearly represents the buyer and another clearly represents the seller (as in a divorce case), there are no hidden or overt conflicts of interest.

You can expect to pay a buyer's broker a fee set in advance or an hourly rate. The fee would be based on prevailing real estate commissions in your area. Hourly rates are typically $50 to $75 an hour. It sounds expensive, but many first-time buyers may prefer to pay their own broker to gain his or her expertise of the housing market, knowledge of financing, and negotiating skills.

To locate a buyer's broker in your area:

- You can tap into a national network by sending $4 and the zip code you want to buy in to: Buyer Broker Network, 1641 Backlick Road, Suite 201, Springfield, VA 22150. You will receive up to three names of brokers who are trained to represent buyers. If there is none in your area, your $4 will be refunded.

- Ask local real estate lawyers, professors, mortgage loan officers, and friends for recommendations.

For more information, you can send for a book, *Buyer's Brokerage: A Practical Guide for Real Estate Buyers, Brokers and Investors,* from The Tremont Press, P.O. Box 2307, Silver Spring, MD 20902, $6.95.

If you do hire a buyer's broker, make sure the broker isn't collecting two commissions: one from you and one from the seller.

When You Are the Seller

You can sell your home yourself or hire a broker to do it for you.

There's one advantage to doing it yourself. You won't have to pay an agent's commission, which could save you thousands of dollars.

But doing it yourself involves a lot of work, including marketing, advertising, and answering prospective buyers' questions. Consider these factors, too: Are you comfortable talking to strangers? Will you be embarrassed to ask potential buyers personal questions about their finances? Is your home located in an easy-to-find spot or would you attract more potential buyers if an agent was driving them around? How adept are you at advising buyers about financing? Even if you can do all of the above, weigh the value of your time against hiring a broker.

And unless you are certain that your house will sell quickly, hire a broker.

Why? A good broker will advertise your house through local and/or national branches; schedule and show your home to potential buyers; help you set the price; assist qualified buyers with financing; and handle paperwork and negotiations related to the sale.

Naturally, those services don't come free. Customary broker-age commissions are 6 or 7 percent of the home's selling price, but they are negotiable. For instance, brokers may cut their commissions if your house is selling for a high price (their work load is the same whether your house sells for $50,000 or $200,000), or is in good condition in a desirable neighborhood, or if you show the house to potential buyers yourself.

Before you hire a broker, ask for referrals from friends and neighbors. Talk to two or three before you hire one. Find out if they specialize in your type of housing—condominiums, coop-eratives, or single-family houses. Your broker should be well versed in financing alternatives and be able to explain them to you clearly.

Be wary of a broker who asks to be paid before the closing on the house, although your broker will expect you to sign a listing agreement, which is a written employment contract between an owner and one or more brokers. (Avoid oral agreements.) Writ-ten agreements usually take one of the following forms, regard-less of whether your home is a house, a condo, or a co-op:

- An exclusive agency. One broker has the right to sell your property for a specified period—typically sixty to ninety days. But if you sell the house yourself during that time you don't have to pay any brokerage commissions.

- An exclusive right to sell. If a sale is made during the period of a listing agreement, you must pay your broker a commis-sion, even if the sale is made by someone other than the broker. This is the most common type of contract and many brokers insist on it. Limit it to sixty days, in case you're not pleased with that broker. You can always extend it.

- A multiple listing agreement. An agreement among brokers to share their listings. It provides for the sales commission to be split between the broker who listed the property and the broker who finds a buyer. It may provide you with the widest exposure to buyers and is the number one reason to use a real estate agent.

- An open listing. You contact real estate companies and tell them you will pay a commission to any broker who sells your house. You retain the right, however, to market the property directly and not pay a commission and to hire additional brokers during the listing period.

An open listing may sound the most attractive because you are not beholden to any real estate agent. But many agents won't show prospective buyers these properties because earning a commission on them is too much of a gamble.

WORKING WITH A REAL ESTATE LAWYER

You will need a lawyer to help you buy or sell a house. Find one through referrals from friends and relatives. Although many real estate brokers make referrals, be careful when the broker represents the seller and you are the buyer. There is a built-in conflict of interest when you use the broker's lawyer. The lawyer may hesitate to raise issues or problems that could impede the sale—and block the broker's commission—and you want your lawyer to raise all potential problems before you agree to the deal.

Conduct interviews and hire the lawyer with whom you feel most comfortable. Ask if the lawyer has expertise in the type of housing you are buying. Will the lawyer have time to meet your deadlines or will most of the work be done by a less-experienced associate? There's nothing wrong with the lawyer delegating work, as long as you are billed at the associate's lower rate.

Ask about fees at your initial meeting. Tell the lawyer you want to be charged an hourly rate, not a flat fee or a percentage of the purchase price of the house. An hourly rate will generally cost you the least. Does the hourly fee include everything or will you pay extra for the lawyer to write the contracts and attend the closing?

Before you close on the house you will be asked to sign a

purchase agreement. Take it to your lawyer and add the inspection clauses you want included. For instance, your lawyer should draft an inspection contingency for the entire house in case, for example, the water pipes are bad. And don't buy a house that is leased, especially if a tenant lives there now, without consulting a lawyer. It may be harder than you think to get the tenant out.

When you buy a condo or co-op, there may be a prospectus or an offering plan containing details about the apartment, the building, the budget, or the rules of the association, written in technical language that your lawyer can decipher and explain. A lawyer can review the real estate contract for quirks and for tax implications of the sale, tailoring it to your needs. Get a separate bill for the tax advice you receive. It is deductible from your income tax in the year you buy the property.

Other deductible expenses when you buy a home: **points** (a fee the lending institution charges for the mortgage) in the year they are paid; and some settlement costs such as interest charges and your portion of real estate taxes paid at closing.

When you sell a home, as long as you are reinvesting the proceeds in a new home within two years, you may deduct the same expenses, with the exception of points. When computing your capital gains tax, however, you may use the points as "selling expenses" to reduce the amount realized from the sale.

After another month of haphazardly looking, Sue and Paul called an agent recommended by friends who had bought a house in one of their favorite neighborhoods.

After a few weekends of visiting properties with Betsy, the agent, she had a clearer idea of what they were looking for and what they could afford.

One evening Betsy showed them a house that had just gone on the market. No one else had seen it yet. Sue and Paul loved the house. The outside needed a paint job and the floors needed refinishing, but otherwise it looked pretty good for a sixty-year-old house. The owners were asking $135,000.

Sue and Paul hired a lawyer and made a bid of $125,000. It was rejected, but they eventually compromised on $131,000.

Both sets of parents pitched in with interest-free loans, helping Sue and Paul make a down payment of $20,000 (15 percent of the house price). After shopping for mortgages, they picked a conventional, fixed rate, thirty-year loan. But choosing a mortgage wasn't easy.

FINANCING YOUR FIRST HOME

Prior to the 1970s, there was only one kind of mortgage; the conventional thirty-year, fixed-rate type. It's simple to understand—you borrow the money to finance your home and pay it back in regular monthly installments for the next thirty years. The monthly payments and interest rate on the loan never change, whether market interest rates move up or down. As your income rises, your monthly payments remain the same. For these reasons, conventional mortgages are still popular.

Ah, for the good old days. Today the world of home financing is a baffling mess of alphabet soup.

Every mortgage contains five features that can be mixed and matched in various combinations to suit your needs. The elements are:

1. The term or length of time it takes to pay off the loan.
2. The initial interest rate of the loan.
3. The principal or amount you owe.
4. The monthly payment.
5. The frequency with which the interest rate and/or the monthly payments can change and the amount it can change.

Combinations of these features form an entire universe of **creative financing**, but we will focus only on those well-suited to young professionals with rising incomes. These include interest rate buy-downs, a device to lower initial mortgage payments; adjustable rate mortgages (ARMs), graduated payment mortgages (GPMs); and growing equity mortgages (GEMs). Equity-sharing, where property is bought under joint ownership, is attractive to people who have little savings for a down payment, but the capability to meet monthly expenses.

Interest Rate Buy-downs

A buy-down is not a mortgage plan, but a subsidy of the mortgage interest rate that lowers the buyer's monthly payments during the early years of the loan. It allows the seller, the buyer, or a third party to pay part of the mortgage interest up front, lowering initial monthly payments, typically for one to three years.

For example, Smith the builder is having trouble selling his new townhouses because interest rates are high—13 percent. To attract more business, he offers a buy-down: If a purchaser buys one of his houses, Smith will buy down the interest rate to 11 percent. To do this, Smith sends the purchaser's mortgage bank a check for, say, $200 a month for three years. Smith will lose money by doing this, but it's better than going bankrupt.

The subsidy that Smith gives the buyer makes the sale possible. But after the buy-down expires the purchaser's monthly payments will increase. Thus, a buy-down is advisable only if you expect your income to rise substantially. But at least initially, the income you need to qualify for a loan is lower. One catch: Make sure that Smith's townhouse wasn't overpriced to start with.

Adjustable Rate Mortgage (ARM)

The interest rate or monthly payment is adjusted up or down periodically (every six months, or every one, three, or five years) with changing market conditions. The rate reflects the interest the mortgage lender must pay to savers and investors. It is determined by an index of U.S. Treasury security rates or the Consumer Price Index or other economic indicators.

Adjustable rate mortgages linked to shorter-term indexes (six-month or one-year indexes) are more volatile than those tied to three-year or five-year indexes. The interest you (the borrower) pay on an adjustable rate mortgage is generally one or two percentage points below what you would pay for a fixed-rate mortgage, to compensate you for the extra risk of unpredictable rates.

Many adjustable rate mortgages have interest-rate or monthly payment caps limiting the amount your payments can increase. These ARMs with caps provide extra protection, but carry a slightly higher interest rate than a pure ARM. Insist on a cap; otherwise, you will have no economic security.

The lender must adjust your rate downward when the index it is tied to declines, but increases are optional and the lender doesn't have to exercise them. However, most lenders do.

The primary advantage to an adjustable rate mortgage is that the interest rate is usually lower than a fixed-rate mortgage. Therefore, your monthly payments will be lower and you will need less income to qualify for the loan.

Graduated Payment Mortgage (GPM)

The graduated payment mortgage is for home buyers who must stretch to afford mortgage payments at first, but can make larger monthly payments later as their incomes rise. The interest rate is fixed, but the monthly payments aren't; payments start out lower than usual and increase gradually each year (about 5 to 7 percent) usually for five to ten years. Then the monthly payments level out.

One drawback of the graduated payment mortgage: it will cost more than a conventional mortgage. Reason: some of the interest payments from the early years are deferred and added to the loan principal, increasing your debt.

Growing Equity Mortgage (GEM)

A growing equity mortgage, also called a rapid payoff mortgage, allows you to pay the mortgage in less than thirty years. The buyer may be able to put less money down, or qualify for a larger loan since there's less risk for the lender on a shorter-term loan. The interest rate is generally a percentage point or two below market rates. But you must be able to handle regular increases in your mortgage payments.

The interest rate is fixed, but your monthly payments increase annually for the first few years or for the life of the loan (generally fifteen years). The changes in the monthly payments are based upon an agreed-upon schedule or an external financial index.

A GEM could be a GPM with a shorter term (fifteen years instead of thirty), but there's one key difference. With a GEM, all the payment increase is applied to the loan principal (not the interest), so you can build equity in the home rapidly, which cuts the total loan costs dramatically. If you can afford the increase in monthly payments, this is a good mortgage to get.

Equity-Sharing

This is the most complicated type of home financing, but it is useful for young professionals with little or no savings who can afford sizable monthly payments and have parents who are seeking tax shelters.

For example, equity-sharing allows Rachel and her parents to buy the condo together and share in its benefits and expenses. Rachel could continue living in her apartment while building **equity**. At the same time, her parents, who are in the 50 percent marginal tax bracket, could shelter income through mortgage and real estate tax payments and **depreciation**.

An equity-sharing deal can be structured in hundreds of ways, but usually the investor (in this case, Rachel's parents) provides part or all of the down payment or a portion of the monthly payments, or both, and receives a proportionate share of the equity when the unit is sold. The investor receives rent from the occupant (Rachel) and can deduct interest, property taxes, and other expenses and depreciate part of the property.

An agreement typically runs for three to seven years, when one of the partners buys out the other or they sell the property to a third party.

As owner-occupant Rachel pays a fair rent to the investor (her parents) on the investor's share of the property. But as part owner, she can deduct interest and taxes, which she can't do as a renter.

Here's how equity-sharing would work on Rachel's $80,000 condominium, with a 12 percent mortgage, an $8,000 down payment, and $2,000 in closing costs split between Rachel and her parents.

Monthly payments for principal and interest on the mortgage are $741. Other monthly costs are $24 for insurance, $90 for property taxes, and $90 for maintenance, or $945. Rachel and her parents each pay $473 of these expenses.

In addition, Rachel pays a fair-market rent on the half of the property owned by her parents ($275) plus the entire utility bill ($40 a month), bringing her total monthly expense to $788. When mortgage interest and property taxes are deducted from her federal income taxes, her net monthly cost is $663, assuming that she's in a 30 percent marginal tax bracket. (She earns $25,000 a year.)

For Rachel's parents, gross monthly costs of $473 are just about offset by the rental payment of $275 they receive from Rachel and substantial tax advantages of $182 a month.

Rachel and her parents agree to end the arrangement in five years. Assuming that the property appreciates at the annual rate of 6 percent, it should net (after paying a 6 percent sales commission) about $99,000—or a gain of $10,000 for each partner before taxes, which is 200 percent of the original $5,000 (each) investment.

Of course, there are risks in equity-sharing. If a property

doesn't appreciate enough by the selling date set by the partners, there will be problems refinancing it. Each partner has less flexibility than if he or she owned the entire property, but that risk is minimized when family members are equity partners.

A contract that anticipates potential problems helps narrow the risks. A legal document outlining the rights and responsibilities of both partners is crucial, especially when deals are struck between family members. Because equity-sharing is a mix of real estate, security, and tax law, both a lawyer and an accountant should review the contract. The following points should be covered:

- Internal Revenue Service requirements. Both partners hold the property as "tenants in common"—a legal term that, in effect, prevents the investor from selling the property from under the owner-occupant. The occupant must pay the investor a fair market rent to cover his or her portion of the property—especially important when the partners are relatives, so the IRS doesn't construe the agreement as a gift or loan. Each party should write his own check to cover the mortgage payments, and the owner-occupant should send the investor a separate monthly rent check. The property must be the principal residence of the occupant.

- A "trigger date" should be set to sell the home to one partner or on the open market. Neither party can force the other to sell before that trigger date.

- Tax deductions and property appreciation. Determine how they will be shared between the partners.

- Repairs and capital improvements. The contract should spell out who is responsible for paying these expenses.

- Rights and responsibilities of either partner in buying out the other partner or in finding a new partner.

- Rights and remedies of each partner in case of default. For example, if either partner misses three monthly payments the other can buy his share, subtracting selling costs and damages from the other's profits.

- Insurance coverage. Determine who pays for coverage or how it will be divided.

SHOPPING FOR A MORTGAGE

Now that you are more familiar with the language of home financing, you can shop for a mortgage.

Start at the bank or banks you use. But don't stop there. Compare terms of various lenders in your area: mortgage bankers, savings and loan institutions, commercial banks, and credit unions, if you are a member.

Ask your real estate broker and lawyer for referrals. They should be knowledgeable about which lenders offer the best terms. If you buy a newly built home, the builder probably can line up financing through a local lender. It may be the best deal around, but check.

Inquire about more than the interest rate on a mortgage. You also want to know the types of loans available; whether you have to pay points (loan charges, each equal to one percent of the mortgage); and if there are prepayment penalties for paying off the mortgage early. The size of your down payment usually affects the interest rate of the mortgage. The bigger the down payment, the lower the rate. Stay away from a mortgage with an acceleration clause, which allows the lender to demand you repay all the money if you break any rules, such as making a payment late. Ask if your mortgage is assumable by a buyer when you sell your home. If interest rates rise by then, you'll have an enormous edge over other sellers.

Recommendations

When shopping for your first home, try to buy the least expensive home you can comfortably live in, in the most expensive neighborhood you can afford. There are no guarantees of home appreciation; you can only gauge what might happen based on past trends. Historically, the most important factor in real estate appreciation has been location.

Finding the best mortgage to suit your individual financial situation takes a lot of homework. Look at any mortgage with the view that your future income will rise, through raises and inflation, and it's normal to stretch to meet your payments initially.

Make sure you understand what your actual mortgage costs will be—monthly and over the life of the loan—before you make any loan commitment. If you take any type of adjustable rate mortgage, compute your costs using best and worst case scenarios. Consider all the following factors:

- The initial interest rate and how often and much it may change.
- The initial monthly payments and how often and much they change.
- The mortgage term and how often and much it may change.
- The index that the rate, payment, or term changes are tied to.

There are great variations in mortgages, so shop around. Compare five to ten different mortgages before you decide.

GETTING OUT OF A LEASE LEGALLY

Ellen and Scott studied their lease carefully. It looked like they were stuck. And Scott's cousin Mitchell, the real estate lawyer, hadn't held out much hope. "It's harder to break a long-term lease than an oral agreement or one that runs month to month," he said.

Mitchell could come up with only one possible loophole, and it sounded weak. He said they could try "constructive eviction," on the grounds that the landlord hadn't done anything to resolve the problem of the noise from their neighbor's band. Constructive eviction allows tenants in some states to move out without notice, and without liability for future rent payments, when the use of their home is substantially impaired by the landlord's failure to do something. For example, courts have ruled that rats in an apartment or housing code violations constitute cause for constructive eviction.

But Mitchell advised them against pursuing this course because proving the case would be difficult and expensive.

"What if we just give notice and walk away? At worst, we would lose our security deposit, right?" Scott asked.

"No, it could be much worse," Mitchell explained. Although state laws vary, generally, if the landlord makes a reasonable effort to rent the unit and he is forced to rent it for less money or for a shorter term than before, the former tenant would be responsible for making up his shortfall. Also, the former tenant (in this case, Scott and Ellen) would be liable for the money the landlord lost from the time they left until he rented it; for his advertising expenses; even for his legal bills if he sued them and won.

Legal ways to get out of your lease do exist, but the amount of leeway you have varies drastically by state. There is no national standard of consumer protection laws for tenants. New Jersey, for instance, offers the most protection and Alabama the least, says Richard E. Blumberg, associate director of the National Housing Law Project in Berkeley, California, and an authority on tenants' rights.

If your lease has no sublet clause, add one before you move in. But if you haven't done that, the best—and cheapest—route is to find a replacement tenant of whom your landlord approves. To establish the reliability of your subtenant, provide financial references. If your landlord grants permission to sublet, obtain the permission in writing.

Drawbacks to subleasing: You are responsible if the subtenant damages the apartment or defaults on the rent; and you are stuck in the middle of any dispute between your landlord and subtenant. Any breach of your lease by you or the subtenant gives the landlord grounds to sue you for damages and eviction. If you are evicted, your subtenant must leave. Try to get a "novation" agreement between you (the old tenant) and the landlord that, in effect, lets you out of the lease and places the responsibility on the new tenant.

If you can't find a subtenant, or your landlord won't agree to it, try negotiating your way out. If tenants are hard to find, offer to pay the landlord the costs of finding a new tenant by advertising in the newspaper or offer cash, part or all of your security deposit, or an extra month's rent.

The most drastic way to break a lease is to claim "constructive eviction" because the landlord hasn't fulfilled his part of the lease agreement (as discussed above). Consider it only if you are desperate, and don't try it without consulting an attorney.

Thanks to the tight rental market in their city, Ellen and Scott's landlord allowed them to sublet—and a friend knew an intern looking for a place. The band wouldn't bother him, he said, because he spent most nights on call at the hospital.

LIVING WITH A ROOMMATE

Whether you rent or buy, many singles find that living with a roommate reduces living expenses and helps combat potential loneliness. Roommates help you establish social ties, especially when you move to an unfamiliar place. But there is a risk. Living with someone you don't get along with is stressful, as Tom discovered early in his working life.

To save money on rent, he moved in with Neil, a friend of a friend whom he had met briefly. After only six weeks their domestic arrangements started to sour, for many reasons. Tom worked nights at the television station and liked to unwind by listening to music when he came home after midnight. That annoyed Neil. At breakfast, Tom would find that Neil had finished the milk or the cereal, but he rarely remembered to buy any on his way home from work. That annoyed Tom. When Neil's sports car was in the shop for repairs—which was often—he expected Tom to drop him off at friends' and run all the household errands. Neil complained that Tom had to be reminded about paying his share of the telephone or utility bill. And so on.

When Tom got his first raise six months later, he found his own place, forfeiting a month's rent so that Neil wouldn't lose money while he looked for a suitable replacement.

To minimize financial and other conflicts with a roommate, work out the following details before you move in:

- Decide whether one or both of you will sign the lease. The person named on the lease is responsible for the entire rent if the other defaults or moves out, or can ask the other roommate to leave at any time. Protect yourself by writing an agreement specifying the responsibilities of each roommate and the terms for splitting up, including how much notice must be given.
- Agree on the division of chores and expenses and put it in writing. Will the person with the larger bedroom pay more rent? Will you clean the house yourselves or hire a maid? However you divide the chores, write it down and post it on the refrigerator door so no one "forgets" to do certain things. If one roommate has a car, will it be shared for shopping and errands—and who will pay for the gas? How will telephone, utility, and food bills be split? Set aside a regular time to pay bills and discuss any domestic problems.
- Will you buy major furniture and appliances jointly? You can't split a bookshelf or a frying pan when one person moves out, so buy each item separately.
- Evaluate your renter's insurance needs. You will need two policies to cover each of your belongings.

7

FINANCIAL ADVISERS

WHEN YOUR FINANCIAL AFFAIRS BECOME TOO complex or you want services and advice beyond the scope of this book, you need a professional financial adviser.

How do you know when that time comes? Generally, single people with incomes of $40,000 or more and married couples with incomes of $60,000 or more should seek expert help. At that point high tax rates influence investment and cash-flow decisions. However, any major life changes—marriage, divorce, having children, buying or selling a home, changing jobs, receiving an inheritance—may trigger a search for professional advice.

Choosing an appropriate financial adviser is no simple task because the services they perform overlap. Sure, some functions are straightforward. You wouldn't ask a lawyer for stock tips or a stockbroker to draw up a will. If you have tax questions, you'd ask an accountant.

But there is another kind of financial adviser with the generic name "financial planner." All kinds of specialists—from insurance agents to tax-shelter salespeople to bona fide financial experts—can and do call themselves by this murky label. Financial planners possess no common background, training, or expertise. They may be commissioned salespeople hawking insurance policies, mutual funds, or tax shelters, or highly competent financial experts who can give you a broader perspective on your overall financial needs and how they interrelate.

The trick is distinguishing the good financial advisers from the chaff. Ask friends and relatives for referrals, particularly if they are in a similar tax bracket and/or occupation. Attend free seminars and lectures conducted by financial planners, stockbrokers, and accountants. You'll find them listed in the business section of your local newspapers. Interview at least three advisers about services and fees before selecting one. You want to feel comfortable with whomever you choose—money is an intimate topic. Look for an adviser whose approach to handling money is consistent with yours, not someone who favors much more or fewer risks.

Always ask the adviser how he or she is paid—by selling advice to clients or through commissions earned on specific products. When you're seeking objective advice you're not likely to find it from someone who earns a commission on particular products.

CHOOSING A STOCKBROKER

Don't try to find a broker by walking into a brokerage unannounced and asking for help. You will be given "the broker of the day," the person on floor duty to open new accounts. Ask for the manager. Say that you are interviewing all the top firms and that you would like to meet the firm's best broker.

Of course, you won't have access to the very top brokers in the firm, especially if you're investing a few thousand dollars. Those brokers devote their time to wealthy clients, whose big accounts generate the most commissions. Still, even with a few thousand to invest, you're entitled to sound advice. If a broker doesn't treat you seriously, go to the next brokerage and the next, until you find someone eager to work for you.

Ask questions. Check credentials—college, specific training, experience. You'll want someone who has been through several market cycles rather than a newly minted trainee, even though a novice broker has more time to devote to you. Don't expect any broker to do everything. You must do your homework—read financial publications and research investment ideas.

Questions to ask when interviewing prospective brokers: How successful has your research department been in picking stocks? How do you make recommendations—is there a guiding philosophy or do you follow other brokers? Do you have an area of specialization—**new issues** or municipal bonds? Do you put your own money behind your recommendations? Is there a flat fee or extra charges for buying stock in **odd lots** (fewer than 100 shares)? When you suggest clients buy a particular stock, do you also recommend a selling price? Ask for names of other clients you may call for references.

The way a broker responds to your questions is just as important as his or her answers. A broker shouldn't make you feel stupid and should be able to explain investments clearly, without relying on jargon.

The broker should ask questions, too, to get a clear picture of your investment goals: How much money do you make? Is yours a two-income family? Does your family have adequate insurance coverage? Are you investing for short-term gains or to build a nest egg to buy your first house? Are you willing to take risks for high, potential gains or do you prefer steady, conservative growth?

Once your account is open you can buy securities at any time. For your first trade, you may be asked to pay part or all the costs up front, depending on your age, credit status, and the size of the transaction. After that, you can generally trade when you want to and pay within five business days.

After you select a broker, be alert to signals of good or bad service. Examples of good service: Does the broker explain complicated entries to you over the phone, rather than send an impersonal letter? Do you periodically receive articles from general and business publications? Do you receive letters thanking you when you open a new account, place an unusually large order, or refer clients? Does your broker repeat your order after executing it to make sure no errors crept in? If there's an error in a transaction, do you get a call from the broker before you discover it yourself? Do you get a concise monthly record of all transactions?

Danger signals that you are not receiving adequate attention: Is your broker too busy to help you when you call? Look for **churning**—excessive transactions netting your broker more in commissions than you receive in profits. Do the recommended investments fit your objectives or are they too risky or conservative? Does your broker misrepresent stocks, promising they will double in six months, or constantly call you with hot tips that don't pan out?

If you suspect your broker isn't working hard enough for you, switch. A broker is your employee. Evaluate your broker's performance annually. You can't expect your broker to be right all the time, but if your portfolio has fared much worse than the Standard & Poor's 500 index, fire your broker. Many experts suggest keeping accounts with more than one broker so you can compare performances. For example, one broker can handle bonds, another blue-chip stocks, and another can track new issues.

The type of firm your broker works for may affect the service:

- National wirehouses such as Merrill Lynch, E.F. Hutton, and Shearson/American Express, with branches across the country, offer a wide range of products from stocks, tax shelters, and money market mutual funds to life insurance, loans, and mortgages.
- Regional firms such as Alex Brown & Sons in Baltimore and Piper Jaffray & Hopwood in Minneapolis, as well as local firms, often spot good local companies before the big firms and may give more personalized attention.
- Discount brokers, local and national, charge lower commissions (as much as 70 percent less than full-service brokers), but don't give services beyond buying and selling stocks at your request. Most discounters don't market new stock is-

sues or tax shelters, or make recommendations, or have research departments. But they can provide access to research material of other firms, including Value Line and Standard & Poor's. When you use a discounter, you don't have an individual broker; whoever answers the phone waits on you. Don't use discounters until you have the confidence and experience to make your own decisions. Small investors who buy stocks in odd lots or low-priced shares don't save much on trades below $1,500 because of minimum commissions charged. If you do use a discount broker, study company earnings reports, read investment newsletters and publications, and call companies and ask questions.

After meeting a stockbroker at a party, Rachel began receiving phone calls from him. It was clear that Andrew was not interested in her romantically; he wanted her business. Rachel told him that she didn't have money to buy individual stocks, but that only encouraged him to call with "hot tips." Finally, in desperation, she told him to stop hounding her and slammed down the phone. He got the message.

Making "cold calls" are part of a stockbroker's business; they are a way of finding new clients. Because many people have difficulty saying no, they end up buying investments they really don't want. Listen to what the caller has to say, but if you don't want the investment, don't hem and haw. It will only encourage the broker to call back. Giving one of these answers immediately should convince the salesperson you are a no-sale:

- All my money is invested and I'm satisfied with what I've got.
- I already have a broker and I don't plan to switch.
- Send me some literature on the investment. If I'm interested I'll call you back. But please don't call me again.
- It doesn't sound right for me. I don't think I'm your kind of customer.

If the caller is selling a special deal that you must buy today, cut off the conversation immediately. No respectable broker would rush an unknown customer into an investment overnight.

SOLVING A DISPUTE WITH YOUR BROKER

If you have a dispute with your broker about the handling of your account, call the broker to resolve it. If that fails, call the branch manager. If you're still not satisfied, write to the president of the brokerage. Then, as a last resort, take your case to arbitration by contacting the customer complaint representative at one of the stock exchanges.

Any investor can take a member of a securities exchange or the National Association of Securities Dealers, Inc., to arbitration.

The arbitration process allows you to seek justice without resorting to an expensive and time-consuming lawsuit. Arbitrators are selected from the top ranks of the securities industry and other fields—corporate chiefs, bankers, academics, accountants, and lawyers. Your case will be heard by one to five arbitrators, depending on the amount in dispute.

Most claims filed against brokers in arbitration involve making unsuitable recommendations or "puffing" the value of a stock; mishandling the mechanics of an account; churning; and account errors, such as when you tell your broker to buy 200 shares when a stock reaches 20, but he buys it for you at 25.

The exchanges have offices in most major cities. For the forms to start the procedures, write:

- National Association of Securities Dealers, Inc., Two World Trade Center, 98th Floor, New York, NY 10048.
- New York Stock Exchange, 11 Wall Street, New York, NY 10005.
- American Stock Exchange, 86 Trinity Place, New York, NY 10006.

All the exchanges require a deposit when you file for arbitration. Generally, if you win the case, the loser must repay the deposit. If the amount in dispute is up to $1,000, the deposit is $15; up to $2,500, the deposit is $25; up to $5,000, the deposit is $100; up to $10,000, the deposit is $200; up to $20,000, the deposit is $300; and up to $100,000, the deposit is $500.

CHOOSING AN ACCOUNTANT

When you interview accountants, be prepared to discuss your assets, liabilities, investment goals, how much risk you want to take, and financial changes you anticipate, such as supporting a parent or receiving an inheritance. Bring along past tax returns. Ask how he would have prepared your past returns differently and for suggestions on future returns. You will generally pay a small fee for the initial appointment.

An accountant should go beyond performing clerical functions. He should be able to describe the personalized services you will receive. For example, it's not enough to calculate whether you should invest in a tax shelter; he should help you select one.

Check an accountant's education and background. A certified public accountant has completed years of training and passed examinations, generally keeps up with the latest tax developments through reading and seminars, and can represent you before the Internal Revenue Service in a dispute (but not in tax court, where you need a lawyer). The "CPA" designation guarantees a level of academic training and practical experience—important factors if you want a sophisticated analysis of your business or personal tax situation. An accountant who isn't a CPA can be equally competent, but it's harder to discern, so don't try. Stick to CPAs.

Ask what type of clients the accountant handles. A large, prestigious national accounting firm, such as one of the "Big Eight" firms, specializes in corporate clients, not individuals, so you would be a low priority. Find a sole practictioner or a local firm that specializes in tax planning for individuals.

Don't be overly impressed by an accountant who says his clients' returns are never audited. It could mean the accountant is too timid to take advantage of justifiable tax breaks. Find out if the accountant uses computers to plan your taxes; it could get the job done quicker and cheaper.

Fees vary. Many accountants bill their time at hourly rates of $50 to $100. Others charge a flat fee; for example, $500 for a complicated tax return. You could pay up to $1,000 a year for tax, estate, and retirement planning.

Signs that indicate your accountant is not providing good service are if you receive notices from the Internal Revenue Service about mistakes; if your tax return is prepared at the last minute, although you have provided information way before the deadline (this applies only when you are owed a refund, not when you owe money); and if instructions to you are hard to follow.

CHOOSING A LAWYER

Generally, ask prospective lawyers these questions, regardless of what the specific case concerns:

- Do you handle cases like mine? If so, how have they turned out, how long did it take to settle them, and what fees were charged?
- Who will do the work, you or less experienced associates, paralegals, and secretaries? There's no problem with subordinates handling the work as long as you're not billed at the experienced lawyer's hourly rate.
- How will I be billed for your time? Lawyers often use a tenth or quarter of an hour as a minimum charge. That may seem petty, but the costs can add up. For example, if the lawyer charges $75 an hour, a three-minute phone call will cost you $7.50 billed to the tenth of an hour; $18.75 billed to the

quarter-hour. Lawyers may charge a flat rate for common procedures such as drawing up a will, or a contingency fee (20 to 50 percent is typical) based on the amount collected when your case is settled. Ask about charges for court, filing, and copying fees.

To check the educational background of a lawyer, consult the *Martindale-Hubbell Law Directory* at your public library.

CHOOSING A FINANCIAL PLANNER

Talk to at least three planners before you select one. Most will meet with prospective clients at no charge for an initial consultation to describe their services. Ask for a breakdown of services and fees, as they vary widely:

- Commission only. Avoid planners who receive compensation only by selling you investments.
- Fee only. These planners charge an hourly fee of $40 to $120 or a percentage (often 1 percent) of your income, with a minimum fee of $750 to $1,000, or a planner may charge you a percentage of your net worth, although that's unlikely unless you're wealthy. For an initial financial plan you may pay $500 to $1,500 and $300 to $500 for a yearly review and update. Ask for specific recommendations to implement through a broker. Otherwise, you're wasting money on expensive advice. If you buy the stocks the planner recommends, use a discount broker; you already paid for the advice.
- Fees and commissions. Most planners are paid through a combination of fees and commissions. They draw up an individual plan, then place investments through a broker or insurance agent and split the sales commissions. You are not obligated, however, to buy the investments recommended by the planner.

Check credentials: How experienced is the planner? Is the planner "certified," which means he or she has completed correspondence courses and passed examinations? The designation "certified financial planner" signifies only that the planner passed the correspondence courses; you may prefer a planner who is a registered investment adviser or has a degree in accounting or law. What are the firm's in-house resources—are there registered investment advisers to analyze investments; estate planning experts; insurance professionals; CPAs; and lawyers available at no extra cost?

Ask the planner to show you a sample plan designed for a client in a similar financial situation (the client's name will be deleted, of course). Ask how many clients the planner handles and their average net worth. If your net worth is considerably lower, you may not get enough attention. Ask the planner for names of other clients for references, as well as for professionals with whom the firm works. Ask the clients how their investments have fared under the planner's advice and whether the planner takes the lead in informing them of changes that affect them.

Once you select a planner, the process begins with a series of meetings. You discuss and define your goals. The planner will produce a formal document called a financial plan based on your responses to questions such as these:

What are your financial problems? What is your income? Is yours a two-income family? What is your tax bill? How much risk do you feel comfortable taking? What fringe benefits do you receive at work? Do you have a will drawn up? Do you own a home? Do you foresee any large expenditures or changes in the future? Is one spouse planning to stay home when you start a family? Planners will ask you to bring along documents such as a copy of your income tax return, insurance policies, charge account statements, checkbook stubs, and retirement fund and investment records.

You generally will need a financial planner when insurance, investment, tax, and legal questions are interrelated and cannot be solved by any one professional. A good planner will contact you regularly and send you information. A planner should advise you, at no charge, on simple questions such as where to invest your Individual Retirement Account or how much to pay for $100,000 of term insurance.

Meet with your planner at least twice a year, including one session around midyear for tax planning. If you wait until October it will be too late to take the appropriate steps to reduce your tax liability.

Each year at your annual review you should see an increase in your net worth through your investments. Look for at least a 12 percent increase (over and above your yearly salary increase). If your investment return is close to what you can get by investing on your own, then your planner isn't doing very well.

A sound financial plan will not favor any one product or service the planner sells or the ones that pay the highest commissions. Young couples should be leery of plans advising them to buy large amounts of whole life insurance—say $500,000 or more—or to invest in limited partnerships before they have bought a home or started Individual Retirement Accounts. These are warning signs that your planner is recommending investments with high sales commissions, regardless of your investment objectives and goals.

You can buy a computerized financial analysis from a bank financial planner, large brokerage house, or insurance company for $100 to $250. But don't. The report can run twenty pages or longer and give you general boilerplate advice. But the quality of the recommendations is generally not very good, especially if it's supplied by an organization with a specific product to sell. Instead, go to an independent planner who gives advice for a fee and doesn't depend on commissions earned by arranging your investments.

To obtain names of planners in your area, contact the International Association for Financial Planning, 5775 Peachtree Dunwoody Road, Suite 120C, Atlanta, GA 30342, and the Institute of Certified Financial Planners, 3443 South Galena, Suite 190, Denver, CO 80231.

8

MONEY AND YOUR JOB

RACHEL HATED TALKING ABOUT MONEY, ESPECIALLY with her bosses. To avoid a painful discussion, she decided to accept whatever raise was offered today at her job review. "No, that's the coward's way out," she chided herself. "If I can negotiate business deals for clients, then I can negotiate a raise."

"Rachel, we think you're doing a fine job for us," said Andrew Taylor later that morning. It was just her luck to have her review done by the partner with the reputation as the biggest tightwad. "We're so pleased with your work we're giving you an 8 percent raise. How does that sound?"

"Just fine, Mr. Taylor," she replied. "I appreciate your confidence in me. I know you won't be disappointed in my work." She got up to leave.

"I guess I'm just a chicken," she confided to her friend Barbara over lunch. "I just accepted the figure he named. I totally caved in. It seemed so undignified to argue about money."

"Well, I hear they're giving out 10 to 12 percent raises this year, so as long as you're on the high end of that, you did all right," Barbara said.

"Oh, where did you hear that?" Rachel asked, trying to sound casual.

"I overheard Patricia and Mary in the ladies' room. They didn't realize I was there. Anyway, Patricia said skinflint Taylor offered her 8 percent—but she got him up to 10 percent. But we know he doesn't think too highly of her work."

Rachel tried to maintain her composure. It really galled her that Patricia would be making more money than she. Patricia was known for doing less than thorough research. "Well, I did okay," Rachel mumbled.

Tom signaled the waiter to bring another round of drinks. It was the least he could do, he thought. He was commiserating with Jim, his best friend, who had been fired abruptly from his job as associate producer at Channel 14. Losing his job hadn't come as a total shock. A new station director had been brought in two weeks ago to boost ratings, and Jim suspected that the new director would want to bring in his own people.

There is no such thing as lifelong job security in broadcast journalism, Tom reminded himself. Still, Jim's predicament underscored his own vulnerability.

"I shouldn't have gotten angry when he told me I was getting axed," Jim said. "If I had stayed calm I could have negotiated a better severance deal. Tom, I don't want you to be paranoid, but there are things you should start thinking about."

"I know. My job hangs by as thin a thread as yours did," Tom said.

Sue walked out of her boss's office, furious. She had asked him why she had been passed over for a promotion and she could hardly believe the reason. Her boss told her she didn't use her expense account enough. Of all the dumb things she had ever heard! The promotion had gone to Mike, who had joined the company a year after her. "Mike seems like a hustler. He goes after new business aggressively by wining and dining prospective clients," she had been told.

Sue thought Mike spent entirely too much time in restaurants and not nearly enough time at his desk. She had bailed him out on two projects in the last three months, and she wasn't the only consultant at the firm who had put in extra hours because Mike had gotten into a crunch.

"Some reward I got for helping him out," she thought. "You would think this company would appreciate someone who displayed a little frugality." Sue hardly ever took clients to lunch because she thought more work could be accomplished in an office—without the distractions of food and drink.

"No more tuna sandwiches for me," she said in anger. "If what they reward around here are padded expense accounts and two-hour lunches, count me in."

IMPROVING YOUR BARGAINING SKILLS

Your attitude about money affects more than your wallet. As Rachel and Sue's situations illustrate, fear of money—discussing it, spending it, and negotiating for it—may affect your career.

Many professionals feel uncomfortable discussing money. We expect our employers to reward us on the basis of merit and hard work—just as in school our intelligence and diligence were rewarded with good grades and other honors. Unfortunately, the business world doesn't work that way. Sometimes the people earning the most money are not the best workers or the smartest. They are simply the best negotiators.

While men and women have trouble bargaining for money at job interviews or at raise time, the problem seems to afflict women more. Despite coming of age in the so-called "liberated" atmosphere of the 1960s and 1970s, many professional women haven't overcome years of childhood conditioning. They still believe, maybe subconsciously, that discussing money is rude, ungracious, and unladylike. Nice girls just don't do it. Such indoctrination causes many highly educated women who earn big salaries to regard their earnings as "pin money" and to cling to the childish notion that a dashing knight will rescue them from their financial woes.

Men and women alike will benefit from sharpening their negotiating skills when they interview for a new position or ask for a raise. The first step is to learn to view the negotiating process in a detached, analytical, unemotional way. Regard the rejection of your original demands impersonally, not as a personal slight, or else, like Rachel, you will be overcome by insecurity. The art of negotiating depends on bargaining and compromise. It is crucial to realize that you will win some and lose some, but without negotiating you probably will lose them all. Improving your bargaining skills requires practice. The time and place to begin is before you even take a job—at your interview:

Before going to a job interview, research the market value of your skills by calling trade associations, employment agencies, executive recruiters, and by asking others who held the job about the going salaries. Go to a library or a bookstore and look up the books and magazine articles that contain detailed surveys listing current salaries by job description, experience levels, and location. Geography is an important factor. For example, a beginning lawyer or management consultant is likely to earn $5,000 to $10,000 more a year in New York City than in Houston.

Delay salary talks until you are sure the employer wants to hire you. Personnel counselors advise waiting until you are called back for a second interview. When asked your salary requirements, discuss them in vague terms, if the employer will let you get away with it; for instance, mid-teens, low twenties, high thirties. Try to get the employer to name specific figures first so you don't overprice or underprice yourself. When you are forced to name a specific figure, swallow, take a deep breath, shoot high, and prepare to negotiate. Keep in mind that it is easier to back off a high figure than to come up from a low figure.

Avoid perpetuating the low-earnings trap. When a prospective employer attempts to pin down your last salary—and you believe you were underpaid—hedge. Emphasize that you expect a salary equal to the responsibilities of the new job, not your former job.

Before you accept a job offer, inquire about the company's raise policy. Make sure the criteria for your salary review are clear. Remember that all future raises and benefits will be based on the starting amount, so don't settle for a low salary in the hope of an enormous raise in six months or a year. You are in the strongest position to negotiate when the company is eager to hire you, not when you are already there.

When you are discussing a raise, always talk in terms of your merit to the company and what you have accomplished to increase profits, productivity, and efficiency—not your personal needs. Employers don't care and don't want to hear about your efforts to buy a house or keep up with your rent increases or about your spouse's difficulty in finding a job.

Once you have a job, if you are disappointed in the size of a raise express it diplomatically. Don't nag your boss—it only makes him or her feel guilty and awkward.

Practice negotiating by thinking about what you want to say and anticipating possible responses. Practice with a friend or in front of a mirror if you think it will help.

EVALUATING A JOB OFFER

There is no standard salary increase to expect if another company offers you a job. The amount will depend on several factors, such as the competitiveness of the job market, your particular skills and experience, and your industry. In some instances, you may be willing to switch jobs for no raise at all, if you think the career opportunities are better. However, personnel experts say that a 20 to 30 percent salary increase would be normal if a company is trying to lure you; if you are unemployed, you would be lucky to get a 10 percent raise. These guidelines are based on the assumption that if you stayed in your old job you would be getting a raise of 7 to 10 percent a year and by leaving you sacrifice certain perquisites and incentives.

Compare the fringe benefits as well as the salary offered, although benefits should not be a strong factor unless there is a big differential between the old and new jobs. Job candidates shouldn't even discuss fringe benefits until an offer has been made; otherwise it seems as though you are more interested in benefits than in the job.

To some extent, it is possible to negotiate fringe benefits as well as salary before you take a job. You are in the strongest position to negotiate then, not after you join a company. The range of perquisites available and the amount of bargaining room you have depends largely on your salary level. At $30,000 to $50,000 annually, perks could include a $2,000 to $5,000 bonus for signing on with the company; relocation expenses, including a house-hunting trip before you move; and a subsidy of continuing education classes. But at this salary level, benefits are usually set by the company with little room for give and take.

The most bargaining play is in the $50,000 to $100,000 salary category. Perks could include a $5,000 to $20,000 bonus for joining the company; relocation expenses, including financial assistance in buying a house; a company car (especially for sales jobs); club memberships; and stock options.

Most young professionals are still far from the $100,000 and up salary stratosphere. When you get there, however, you can look forward to the many perks that go along with the job, including personal financial counseling, estate planning, first-class travel, and substantial stock ownership plans.

Naturally, your value to the company is crucial to your negotiating success. The best route is to ascertain the value of your job skills and what they command at other companies. Call your professional organization for advice or speak to executive recruiters in your field. You will always have to overcome your employer's reluctance to grant perks because they can arouse jealousies among workers. A cash bonus is a handy device for settling disagreements about your compensation package. For example, if an employer says that granting your demands will mean giving others the same plums, ask for the difference in an up-front cash bonus. Cash is less visible to your colleagues than a company-leased car you park in the office lot.

Get the details of your compensation package—salary and perks—in writing, stating the date the agreement takes effect. A written document will prevent misunderstandings later and protect you if the person with whom you have negotiated leaves the company. When there's no formal employment contract, a letter will suffice.

SPENDING YOUR COMPANY'S MONEY

Sue's surprise at being denied a promotion because she failed to use her expense account properly is not uncommon. Many professionals don't realize that success in business often depends on finesse in using an expense account to line up potential clients and reinforce vital business relationships. In many industries, for example, sales, public relations, advertising, consulting, entertainment, publishing, and journalism, entertaining is an essential part of conducting business.

For this reason, business lunches are deductible on corporate income taxes. Not using expense accounts properly can harm a career instead of bringing you praise for frugality. Your employer is apt to be more concerned about your failure to develop and nurture contacts than your ability to save pennies.

Of course, you don't want to develop a reputation for abusing expense account privileges. There are no dollar guidelines for using an expense account. It depends on your job responsibilities and your company's attitude. To gauge your company's unwritten code, observe how your colleagues use their expense accounts. Note who uses them, and where and how often other people at your level and immediately above it entertain.

Learn the art of spending money. In some companies it is perfectly acceptable to charge books that will help you in your work; memberships to professional organizations that will increase your visibility; a briefcase or desk accessories. Entertaining business associates with a dinner or cocktail party at your home may be another legitimate expense.

Don't neglect to ask your company to reimburse you for acceptable business expenses just because they are small. They add up. Jot down what you spend on phone calls, newspapers, tips, and other incidentals. Taxi fare home may be reimbursable if your job requires staying late.

Watch what colleagues do to overcome common misunderstandings about whether it is acceptable to take a friend to lunch. The line between friends and business contacts is murky. If you do take a friend out, discuss business at some point. Frequent lunch dates with a person only remotely connected to your business may arouse suspicion.

Using an expense account properly is so important you may overlook its significance instead of heeding an implicit warning. For example, if you are challenged on an expense account, it could be a sign that your integrity is in question and you are in deep trouble with your boss, so get to the root of the problem immediately.

Again, professional women may experience more trouble using expense accounts than their male counterparts. From an early age boys are taught how to make decisions about money and are granted more freedom to control money, while girls are taught how to hunt bargains. As a result men grow up more confident about spending money—their own and their employers'. Another reason women spend less than men on expense accounts is that some men, uncomfortable about women picking up the tab, still dive for the check. For the sake of avoiding a scene, women often acquiesce. Women who anticipate this problem can talk to the maître d' before the meal or arrange to have the bill sent directly to their office.

THE FINANCIAL ASPECTS OF GETTING FIRED

Tom's empathy with his unemployed friend underscored the vulnerability of his own job. The mere thought of unemployment is depressing, and no one likes to dwell on unpleasant thoughts. But if you plan ahead, you can take financial steps—before and after losing a job—that will make doing without a paycheck easier. There's no need for paranoia, but the likelihood of having your job eliminated should be part of your planning. If you think your job is threatened or your company is in financial trouble, take these steps before you get a pink slip.

- Research company policy regarding laid-off workers. Check benefits: severance and vacation pay, extension of health insurance, temporary office space, and outplacement counseling. Outplacement is a euphemism for counseling fired executives.
- After learning the benefits, calmly negotiate a strong severance arrangement. You can turn your employer's guilt and fear about firing you to your advantage. Most companies are concerned about maintaining a good image and employee morale, and may be willing to sweeten the deal. The worst thing to do is to react angrily and storm out of the office without discussing severance pay.
- Build a network of professional contacts that will enable you to hear of job opportunities regularly. Be active in trade organizations. It sounds opportunistic, and it is, but invite people who may be able to help you in the future for lunch or drinks. Ask contacts for career advice before it is obvious that you need it.
- Start budgeting beyond the next month or two. A rule-of-thumb, according to personnel experts, is that you will be out of work one month for every $10,000 you earn annually. Build your reserve funds by cutting your expenses and postponing major purchases until your job is more secure.
- If you are considering a switch to a field with more opportunities, or if you want additional education to make yourself more marketable, enroll in night school or a training program.
- Schedule dental and medical work covered by your employer's insurance plan.

- Consider how you would present your achievements to a prospective employer. Many people who are at the same job they took after graduation don't know how to highlight their skills or write a decent résumé. Get help from friends or professionals.

The above steps will put you in a stronger position in case you lose your job. After the ax has fallen, take these steps:

- Don't take severance pay in a lump sum if, by receiving it over weeks or months, you will keep benefits such as health and dental insurance. When your coverage ends, buy group health insurance—which is cheaper than an individual policy —through your professional society or trade group. Inquire if the company will pay you for any unused sick or vacation days.
- Request outplacement services from your company. Outside personnel experts, hired by your company, can help you prepare a résumé, coach you for job interviews, and provide office space, telephone, and clerical help to track job leads.
- Freelance your skills. Many professions—marketing, accounting, editing, consulting—use free-lancers for part-time or temporary workers.
- If you own your apartment or house, you can use it to raise cash in an emergency. Refinance your mortgage or take out a second trust, which is a six-month to three-year loan secured by your property. You are trading higher monthly mortgage payments for available cash.
- Borrow against your life insurance policy. If you don't have an insurance policy, you can ask a friend or relative to borrow money for you. Make it a business deal. For example, the relative can borrow money from a policy at 10 percent and you can pay it back at 12 percent, which is still well below the market rate for personal loans. Many insurance policies were written when interest rates were low; thus,

borrowing is permissible at lower rates than those offered by commercial lenders.

- Negotiate credit payment schedules. In many cases, creditors will reduce your payments until you find a job. They are understanding because they know if you get into deep trouble, they never will be repaid.

- Cash in any retirement program benefits. You can have immediate use of the money, and you are still far from retirement. Consult an accountant for advice because you may able to income average or defer tax payments. As long as you are looking in the same line of work, job-hunting expenses are tax-deductible—so keep good records.

- Don't let embarrassment or pride prevent you from filing for unemployment compensation. State laws vary, but you can generally collect it if losing the job wasn't your fault. The amount of benefits depends on the state in which you live, how long you worked, and your past salary. You don't pay any taxes on employment benefits, but you can't collect unemployment at the same time you collect severance pay.

EVALUATING A JOB MOVE TO ANOTHER CITY

Within a month Jim got a job offer from a television station 500 miles away. The job title, "associate producer," was the same, but it paid $4,000 a year less. Jim wanted to reject the offer immediately, but his wife encouraged him to investigate further.

The cost of living, tax rates, and prevailing wages differ from place to place. Pay scales for the same job can vary by more than $5,000 a year, while living expenses can vary by 10 percent or more. Before moving to another city for a new job or a transfer or to start a business or professional practice, research the prospective location.

Ask people you know for help. Call someone you know who

lives in the city you are considering. If you don't know anyone, look for contacts through church or professional organizations.

Another good source of free advice is the U.S. Chamber of Commerce. Local chambers can supply names and telephone numbers of agencies that offer specific economic and housing information for their area. Some chambers have jointly published a quarterly called "Inter-City Cost of Living Index," which gives comparative figures for almost 300 cities, including housing, food, utilities, transportation, and health-care costs—but not tax rates. However, there are independent taxpayers' organizations in about forty states, almost always with headquarters in the state capital.

Check the job, housing, and merchandise advertisements in local newspapers to get an idea of prices. For example, by checking the local newspaper, Jim discovered that housing prices were much lower in the new city. He could buy a comparable home for $10,000 to $30,000 less or buy a bigger home than the one his family now had. Jim confirmed this information with local real estate agents when he visited the new city. Check bookstores and libraries for any of the books priced for the mass market that rate the quality of life and cost of living in different areas.

Visit the proposed location at the worst time of the year—e.g., the Sunbelt in the summer—to see all the drawbacks before you move.

Jim and his wife took a short trip to the new city. They looked up an old college friend who lived there and he filled them in on desirable neighborhoods and school districts. Jim had another interview at the television station and was pleased about opportunities for advancement there. Jim and his wife talked to several real estate agents and looked at houses. Lower housing and other living costs would more than compensate for Jim's $4,000-a-year pay cut, so they decided to move.

9

RETIREMENT

"RACHEL, HAVE YOU SET UP YOUR INDIVIDUAL
Retirement Account yet?"

Rachel stopped chewing on her salad. Every time
she had lunch with her ex-boyfriend Mark, he lectured her on
managing her money. "To tell you the truth, I haven't gotten
around to it yet."

"What are you waiting for? If you make a $2,000 contribu-
tion, it will cut your taxes by almost $1,000."

"I know that, but once I put $2,000 in an IRA, I can't touch
it without paying a 10 percent withdrawal penalty. What if I need
the money before retirement to buy a car or a bigger place?"

"Surely you can afford to save for retirement and other things
at the same time? Well, maybe not. I keep forgetting that your
law firm doesn't give the most generous bonuses."

Paul couldn't wait to tell Sue about the job offer. What an
opportunity! Eggplant Electronics was smaller and less established than his company, but it was growing rapidly. Eggplant
had a reputation for being progressive, and his interview did
nothing to contradict that view—the personnel manager who
interviewed him was wearing a sweatsuit and running shoes.
Also, the money sounded terrific—$55,000 a year—and the job
would be challenging. Paul would be in charge of a division with
forty engineers.

He had just one qualm about taking the position. Eggplant had no pension plan. Quitting his job after eight years would mean losing his pension—and he was only two years short of vesting.

Roy knew one of the advantages of setting up his own practice next year was opening a KEOGH plan to shelter income and put money aside for retirement. But that didn't solve his immediate problem—what should he do this year about retirement savings? He wasn't self-employed yet, so he couldn't open a KEOGH plan. Did it pay to open an Individual Retirement Account? The $2,000 annual limit was paltry compared to KEOGH limits. Maybe the best thing to do was nothing—just wait until next year.

PLANNING FOR RETIREMENT

Accumulating money for retirement is probably a low priority —beneath buying a home or educating your unborn children. The best time to start planning for a comfortable retirement, however, is thirty or thirty-five years in advance. The earlier you begin, the more flexibility you have to meet your goals.

There are three sources of retirement income: Social Security, a private pension plan if you are fortunate enough to have one, and your own savings. Given the constraints of the first two sources, you should plan on shouldering much of the economic burden yourself.

How much will you need in retirement? At your age now, it's difficult to tell without knowing how your career will turn out and your future family responsibilities. But let's take a closer look at the impact of present savings choices on your retirement income.

Social Security

When you retire, become severely disabled, or die, you or your beneficiaries will receive Social Security benefits. The money for the benefits comes from Social Security taxes paid by you and your employer during your working life. The amount of tax you pay is determined by your income. To cover the $194 billion in benefits that will be paid out in 1985, workers and employers will each pay up to $2,771 in Social Security taxes per worker. By 1998 the maximum tax is expected to rise to $3,488 —and continue to escalate every year.

Despite speculation that the Social Security system won't be around by the time today's young professionals retire, the popularity of the program—it's probably the nation's favorite—makes that unlikely. Politicians will fear that any action they take to reduce benefits will be perceived as hurting the elderly. So you can count on Social Security benefits to be around when you hang up your briefcase, but maybe not to the extent that today's retirees rely on it.

The biggest misconception about Social Security is that the money deducted from our paychecks now goes into a fund labeled with our own names and sits there until we collect it. On the contrary, Social Security is a "pay-as-you-go" system. Taxes paid in today by workers and employers are paid out immediately in benefits to retired workers. In effect, your payroll taxes are supplementing the financing of your parents' and grandparents' condominiums in Florida.

Thanks to increases they have received based on inflation rates, the benefits for today's retirees far exceed their contributions to the system. For instance, the maximum yearly benefit in 1984, if both spouses worked from 1937 through 1983, was $16,872. Each would have paid in $19,328.39, which means that in only two and a half years their benefits will exceed their contributions. And the average retired couple, if both spouses worked, collected $13,008 in 1984, which means they will surpass their total contributions in just twenty-one months.

If low birth rates continue, however, by the time today's young professionals are ready for Palm Beach, fewer workers will be paying into the system to support more retirees, thus translating into less generous benefits for all. Whether politicians ultimately deal with the problems facing Social Security by reducing benefits or raising taxes, one thing remains certain: We should not count on the government as our sole source of retirement income.

But as long as the Social Security system remains sound, you can expect it to replace 20 to 30 percent of your after-tax income, up to the maximum limit. Currently, the maximum payout is $8,500 per year—and the maximum figure should rise with inflation, so you will probably receive the equivalent of $8,500 of today's dollars in purchasing power. For most retirees, benefits are not taxed! (Social Security income is presently not taxable unless your total income plus nontaxable interest plus one half of your Social Security benefits exceeds $25,000 if single, $32,000 if married.)

Company Pension Plans

If you work for a company that has a pension plan, you're lucky. Less than half the non-government workers in the United States are covered by a private pension plan. What's more, being covered doesn't mean you'll collect those benefits.

The major obstacle to collecting a private pension is called "vesting." It takes a certain number of years—typically ten—before a worker's pension rights "vest" or become guaranteed. Once you vest you can collect the benefits at retirement even if you switch jobs.

Before the 1974 Employee Retirement Income Security Act (commonly known as ERISA), a company could dangle the promise of retirement benefits in front of you and then fire you at age 64, a year before you could collect it. Now that practice is illegal. But ERISA's promise of full vesting turns out to be a hollow one for many mobile workers. The pension system rewards the worker who stays put for thirty years or more, not the ambitious go-getter who switches jobs more often. For instance, if you work at three companies for ten years each, your pension is funded equally by Company A, Company B, and Company C. But the partial pensions from Company A and Company B are based on your final salary when you left those jobs, not your final salary at Company C. Assuming that inflation and job advances pushed your salary up each year, your benefits will be considerably lower than those for someone with an identical salary history who worked at any of those companies for the entire thirty years.

Even if your company goes bankrupt—or your pension plan is otherwise terminated before you collect it—your benefits are federally insured by the Pension Benefit Guaranty Corporation. But there are annual limits on the amount of insurance each worker receives (for example, the 1985 limit is $20,244), and high earners with generous pensions aren't fully insured.

This information may come as a surprise to you. After all, most of us stuff our unread company pension plans in a bottom drawer. Either we can't fathom the thought of aging or we are counting on a buried treasure turning up in the backyard. For reasons as irrational as these, we remain ignorant of the important formulas that determine how well we'll live in our old age. Take your pension plan out of the drawer for a lesson on how to read it.

Most plans base benefits on how long you have worked for the company multiplied by a percentage of your base salary in your final working years. For example, a typical plan may define final earnings as your average salary for the last five years you worked. Then, 2 percent of that figure is multiplied by the number of years of service to the company up to a maximum of thirty years or so. Next, an amount equal to half your annual Social Security benefit is subtracted. Thus, using this formula, a twenty-year employee whose average final earnings were $30,000 and whose Social Security benefits are $700 a month (roughly the maximum) would compute benefits this way:

Six hundred dollars (2 percent of $30,000) multiplied by 20 (years of service) equals $12,000, minus $4,200 (half of yearly Social Security benefits of $8,400) equals $7,800. Therefore, the worker would receive a total company pension (taxed) of $7,800 a year. In addition, the worker would receive total Social Security benefits (untaxed) of $8,400, bringing the total annual pension benefit to $16,200.

A pamphlet that can help decipher your plan is "A Guide to Understanding Your Pension Plan" (1346 Connecticut Avenue, NW, Room 1019, Washington, DC 20036, $2). Karen Ferguson, author of the guide and director of the Pension Rights Center, a public interest group, offers the following tips for reading your company pension plan:

- Before you read the plan, jot down these questions and look for the answers as you read: Am I covered by my pension plan now? If I stop working today will I have earned the right to a pension at retirement? How much would my pension be worth if I stopped working today, at age 65, or at the plan's earliest retirement age, or if I'm married when I retire and want to provide a pension for my spouse? Is my pension fully insured? Will my spouse receive anything if I die? Write down the answers.
- Pay attention to the formula used to figure benefits. Are Social Security benefits subtracted from your pension? If you change jobs after you are vested, are the benefits based on your earnings at the time you leave or is there a cost-of-living increase?

After you understand the basics, you'll know which benefits you will receive. You have the right to ask your company for an individual benefits statement—how much your benefits are worth now and a future projection. Of course, you won't know whether you will stay at the company long enough to collect them. Thus, you will probably want to have a more secure source of retirement income.

Company Profit-Sharing Plans

In addition or as an alternative to pension plans, many companies set up profit-sharing plans for their employees. Typically, the employer contributes an amount equal to a percentage of each worker's salary. The contribution varies each year: it may be 3 percent, or 10 percent, or zero, if the company had a bad year. Employees contribute nothing.

As long as you meet the company's vesting requirements, you may take the money in your plan when you leave, a particularly attractive feature to employees who plan on switching jobs. Vesting schedules are usually much shorter than for pension plans. Generally, you are 20 percent vested after one year of service and fully vested after five years. Watch the vesting schedules! It would be foolish to leave the company a month or a week before you are fully vested.

RETIREMENT SAVINGS PLANS

The most popular retirement savings plan is an **Individual Retirement Account**. An IRA is not one particular investment product, but a shell for any assortment of investments you select. Anyone who earns a salary may set up an IRA—and for almost all young professionals it is too good to pass up. An IRA combines tax deductions and tax deferral, allowing you to shelter income from taxes and build up retirement funds at the same time.

The tax-deduction feature means that if your taxable income is $30,000 and you contribute $2,000 annually, you will be taxed only on $28,000—cutting your tax bill substantially. Tax deferral means the earnings on your IRA will not be taxed until withdrawal, allowing your earnings to compound until retirement.

For example, if you made an annual IRA contribution of $2,000 for 35 years and your investment yielded 8 percent, it would grow to $372,204 ($70,000 savings plus $302,204 interest). You must pay taxes when you withdraw IRA money—between the ages of 59½ and 70½—when, presumably, your tax bracket will be lower. Without an IRA, assuming you are in a 40 percent bracket, your $2,000 savings would be taxed, leaving you with only $1,200 to invest each year. After 35 years at 8 percent, and lacking the IRA's tax-deferral feature, it would grow to only $108,991. Unlike an IRA, however, it wouldn't be taxed at withdrawal.

Restrictions on IRAs are few. You cannot invest more than $2,000 a year (the limit is $2,250 if your spouse does not work). A working couple can contribute $2,000 each in separate accounts. You can open any number of IRAs in any investment you choose as long as the annual contribution doesn't exceed $2,000. For example, you can buy a $1,000 savings certificate, invest $500 in stocks, and another $500 in a mutual fund for your IRA, all in the same year. Unless you are disabled, if you withdraw the money before age 59½ you pay a 10 percent penalty levied by the Internal Revenue Service, plus any additional penalties levied by the institution holding the account.

Don't let the withdrawal penalty discourage you. It isn't always that harsh. For people whose tax brackets are 30 percent or higher, an IRA investment held for six to ten years and yielding 8 to 10 percent a year can outperform other savings plans.

IRA holders are allowed to take physical possession of the money only once a year and it must be re-invested within sixty days. But you can move your money among investments as often as you wish, as long as investment trustees handle the transactions.

You may contribute to your IRA until the April 15 following the tax year. The amount you contribute is flexible—it can be $2,000 one year, $247 the next year, or not one penny.

How much money can you expect in retirement if you invest $2,000 in an IRA every year for 35 years? We mentioned earlier that if you invested $2,000 for 35 years in an IRA at 8 percent interest, your investment would grow to $372,204. That sounds like a fortune, but don't think your money problems are over! If inflation averaged 6 percent over the 35 years, then in today's dollars your $372,204 really would be worth much less.

Figure retirement investments in today's dollars. This has been done for you in Table 9:1. To use this table, estimate how much

rcent Investment Return Above Inflation	Amount in 35 Years If $2,000 Is Invested Annually*	Annual Income If Used Over—	
		15 years	20 years
0	$70,000	$4,667	$3,500
2	$101,989	$7,937	$6,237
4	$153,196	$13,778	$11,272
6	$236,242	$24,324	$20,597

ll numbers are in today's dollars. Thus, we have assumed that IRA limits will be reased beyond $2,000 to match inflation and that you contribute the equivalent of ,000 in today's dollars each year.

your investment returns beat the inflation rate. For instance, if your money market investments return 8 percent and inflation is 6 percent, then your investment return is 2 percent above inflation. With long-term bonds and stocks you may be able to get returns of four to six percentage points above inflation.

For example, Table 9:1 shows that if you saved $2,000 per year in today's dollars in an IRA for 35 years and your return averaged 2 percent above inflation, you would end up with $101,989 in today's dollars. If your return was 4 percent over inflation, you would have $153,196 in today's dollars. The table indicates the annual income your IRA would provide if you spent the money in equal amounts over 15 or 20 years. If during the years you accumulated it, your IRA investment averaged 2 percent above inflation and you could maintain the same 2 percent return after you started withdrawing the money, then you would have $6,237 per year for 20 years. If your investment returns were 4 percent above inflation, you would have $11,272 per year for 20 years. All your IRA money will be taxable upon withdrawal, but your tax rates are likely to be lower than during your working life.

To see how an IRA fits into your total retirement plan, let's review the earlier example of a person who retires with a company pension plan and the maximum Social Security benefit. He would receive $16,300 a year. But if the same person contributed $2,000 a year (in today's dollars) to an IRA for 35 years, with an investment return averaging 2 percent above inflation, he would receive $6,237 more each year.

As shown below, these are the annual amounts from the three sources he would receive in retirement (in current dollars):

Total company pension (taxable)	$7,80(
Total Social Security	8,40(
Use of funds from IRA savings, when drawn over twenty years (taxable)	6,23:
Total annual funds	$22,43:

You would have to pay taxes on the pension distribution plus the IRA distribution. Under current law, there would be no tax on Social Security at this level of income (see page 160). So the total taxable income would be $14,037 (pension, $7,800 plus IRA, $6,237). At 1984 tax rates the tax would be $1,808. Thus, your total available funds from all sources would be $22,437 minus a tax of $1,808, or $20,629.

Choosing an IRA Investment Vehicle

To open an IRA, you must choose among the many institutions vying for your money. Banks, savings and loans, money market funds, mutual funds, stock brokerages, and life insurance companies all offer IRAs.

You should choose an IRA using the same criteria as any other investment you make—but with two exceptions. Because the returns on your IRA are not taxed until withdrawal, there's no advantage to buying a tax-exempt investment such as municipal bonds. And you may be willing to consider IRA investments with higher risks and less liquidity than you normally require because you're not planning to touch the money until you retire.

The type of IRA you buy should be based on these factors:

- Do you prefer slow steady growth or more risk and high-growth potential?
- Will you contribute the maximum $2,000 a year?

- Do you have the time, knowledge, and desire to actively manage your accounts?
- What other investments do you have?
- How important is flexibility? IRA money put in a mutual fund family can be moved in and out of money market funds, stocks, and bonds. You do not have that option with a bank IRA. But you can open as many IRAs as you want, as long as your total IRA investments don't exceed $2,000 a year, so with a little effort you can overcome that disadvantage.

Different types of IRA accounts are characterized by the following features (the various investments are discussed in greater detail in the investment chapter):

- Mutual fund IRAs. An IRA in a stock mutual fund is a good way to capitalize on long-term growth in the stock market. Because IRA money is for the long haul, you may be willing to tolerate year-to-year market volatility in exchange for potentially high appreciation. Bond mutual fund IRAs can provide high guaranteed-interest rates, but you still risk capital losses due to changing interest rates. Money market mutual fund IRAs, although not federally guaranteed, appeal to conservative investors because funds are generally invested in short-term securities, which are virtually risk-free.
- Banks, savings and loan, and trust company IRAs. Funds are usually invested in fixed- and variable-rate certificates of deposit. These are well suited to conservative investors because the accounts are insured up to $100,000. You can also open an IRA in an insured bank money market deposit account.
- Self-directed IRAs with a stockbroker. These are best for sophisticated investors who follow the market. Transaction costs are high, so accumulate at least $10,000 in another

IRA before opening one. You can buy and sell stocks, bonds, certificates of deposit, mutual funds, money market funds, annuities, and limited partnerships, but the risks on your investments can be high.

- Insurance company annuity IRAs. An annuity is a promise by an insurance company to pay you income as long as you live in return for a lump sum investment. The amount the insurer pays each year depends on your life expectancy and the amount you invest. Insurance companies offer IRA annuity plans that generally pay you a constant stream of money from your retirement until death. These annuities pay a guaranteed rate of interest competitive with long-term bond rates. The drawbacks: The insurance company will charge you penalties for early withdrawal on top of the regular IRA early withdrawal penalty. Service fees and commissions are generally higher than on other IRAs. Avoid these. If you want an annuity, let your IRA funds accumulate in another type of IRA investment until retirement and then buy one.

Alternatives to IRAs

An IRA has many advantages as a tax shelter and is well suited to the needs of most young investors, but an IRA is not for everyone. For instance, if your first priority is to buy a home, and you're planning to withdraw the money in just a few years, an IRA isn't wise. If your income is very low, the deductions and tax-deferral features of the IRA will not do you much good. If your income is very high, a tax deduction limited to $2,000 is not going to shelter much income.

In these limited cases, alternate savings plans would be preferable, although if you have enough savings, you can set up an IRA in addition to any of these other plans:

- **KEOGH** plans for the self-employed. KEOGHS are similar to IRAs, but you can make higher contributions: generally up to 20 percent of your income, not to exceed $30,000 (for 1984 and after). KEOGHS are not taxed as heavily as IRAs, because if you withdraw all your retirement money at once, you can use ten-year forward averaging, which allows the withdrawal to be taxed as if it were received in equal parts over ten years. With another type, a defined benefits KEOGH, you set aside an annual sum as high as 50 percent of your self-employment income to meet your retirement income goal.

- Tax sheltered annuities or 403(b) plans. Teachers, hospital nurses, clergy, and other employees of nonprofit organizations are eligible for tax-sheltered annuities (TSAs). In a typical plan, your employer would deduct at least 16⅔ percent of your gross salary, with limits based on your earnings and length of service, and invest it, untaxed, in an annuity. The account belongs to you and generally accompanies you when you switch jobs. Like IRAs, earnings are tax-deferred until withdrawal. Unlike IRAs, TSA money may be withdrawn early without penalty, and there is no maximum age for withdrawal. TSAs are offered by life insurance companies and other employer trusts. Another type of TSA, called a 403(b)(7), follows the same formulas except that employees may invest in mutual funds.

- Salary reduction plans or 401(k) plans are named after the section in the Internal Revenue Service code that permits them. Many companies offer 401(k) plans, allowing employees to defer from 1 to 16 percent of their earnings each year. The money is put in an investment trust that buys stocks or earns a fixed income or is invested in the company's stock. You pay no federal taxes on the money set aside, allowing the earnings to accumulate, tax-deferred, until withdrawal. Unlike IRAs, you contribute before Social Security and state taxes are deducted from your earnings. Another advantage over an IRA is that there are no early withdrawal penalties. In fact, many companies allow "hardship withdrawals" to buy a house or pay medical bills or college tuition for your children, but when the IRS final 401(k) regulations are issued, the rules will be stricter. Many companies match employee contributions, adding 25 to 50 cents for every employee dollar. When the money from the plan is withdrawn in a lump sum, you can reduce taxes by using the ten-year forward averaging method.

- Company thrift or savings plans. In a typical plan, employees contribute from 1 to 6 percent of their after-tax income to an investment program in stocks and other securities. Each employee dollar is matched by an untaxed company contribution of 25 cents or more. If a company matches at least 10 percent of your investment, it's probably a better deal than an IRA, so contribute the maximum amount before opening an IRA. There's no withdrawal penalty if you need the money before you retire and ten-year averaging if you withdraw it. Usually, however, you won't receive the company's contribution until you have worked there at least three years, a drawback if you are planning to leave.

- Incorporation. Before recent changes in the tax laws made KEOGHs and corporate plans equal, doctors, lawyers, and other professionals incorporated to take advantage of incorporation's extensive fringe-benefit opportunities. But with the equal tax treatment of KEOGHs and corporate plans, incorporating may not be worth the extra costs involved. Consult a tax professional for advice tailored to your situation.

Rachel waited in the bank line to deposit her paycheck and annual bonus check. She saw a sign advertising thirty-month savings certificates with 13 percent yields for IRA accounts.

"I'm here and I have my $700 bonus, so I may as well open an IRA with $1,000," she thought. "That will show Mark. I'll be more frugal this month and pay less money on my charge account bills to make up the $300. I can contribute another $1,000 when I save it."

In this case, even though Rachel pays 18 percent interest on her outstanding charge card bill, she is still better off opening an IRA account. Reason: the IRA yield of 13 percent (tax-free) is equivalent to a 20 percent (taxable) return, so she'll come out ahead. And in her 38 percent tax bracket, her $1,000 IRA contribution will cost her only $650 in after-tax dollars because she gets a tax savings of $300.

By making part of her IRA deposit early in the year, that money compounds for a longer time.

"Maybe Sue has a point," Paul thought. He couldn't understand her lack of enthusiasm over his job offer. But after a careful reading of his benefits plan—no easy task—he had discovered that if he quit now, instead of waiting two more years, he would lose $14,000 in retirement benefits.

He wasn't unhappy at work, so maybe Sue was right. Retirement was more than thirty years off, but why throw away benefits he had worked toward for eight years?

Roy was about to send a $2,000 check to his stock mutual fund. Then he realized that it would be smarter to open a new account, using the stock mutual fund for his IRA.

The transaction was easy—the fund had already sent him the IRA form he needed. Sure, $2,000 wasn't much income to shelter compared to KEOGH limits. But in his 45 percent bracket, he could still save $900 in taxes. Certainly that was worth the five minutes it would take to fill out the extra form. He liked investing in a growth stock fund IRA because of its potential for long-term appreciation. And if he wasn't pleased with the fund's performance, he could switch the IRA money into another fund within the same mutual fund family simply by making a phone call.

10

FINANCIAL TRANSITIONS

LIVING TOGETHER

AFTER SIX MONTHS OF DATING, TOM AND JOAN decided to move in together. The topic had come up unexpectedly because Joan's roommate accepted a job offer in another city.

"You know we've spent days discussing what living together will do to our relationship," Joan said. "Don't you think we should spend a couple of hours talking about our money situation?"

"You really have the mindset of a lawyer," Tom joked. "What's there to discuss? We earn roughly the same salary, so we'll split everything down the middle." Actually, Joan earned $8,000 more, but Tom didn't like to dwell on it.

"We need a more organized system. Sit down—I'll show you what I have in mind."

Before setting up a household, a couple should discuss and plan their financial arrangements. Money—how we spend it, save it, and feel about it—is a subject laden with emotions and a source of conflict in relationships. Both partners should recognize differences in their attitudes and make adjustments before problems arise. Resolve these issues before moving in together:

Ownership of Assets

The first and last rule is to keep things separate to avoid legal messes if you split up. For example, if you have a credit card in your name, don't authorize your partner to use it, because you would be responsible for any shopping sprees. Forget buying a home together unless you're planning to marry immediately. If you take a mortgage you are equally liable for it—and if your mate skips out, you're stuck with the payments.

Buy Major Purchases Independently

You can't divide a dining room table or a couch. Neither Tom nor Joan, for instance, owned a coffee table or kitchen chairs and table. So Tom bought the coffee table and Joan bought the kitchen set.

If you feel that you absolutely must buy a house together, you should have a predetermined buy-out formula in case you break up. The deal can be structured as a partnership agreement, allowing one partner to buy out the other's share if the relationship ends or if one partner dies. When you're not married, a good financial planning technique is for each partner to take out a term insurance policy on the life of the other partner, and name yourself as the beneficiary. For example, if Tom and Joan should buy a $100,000 townhouse, each should take out a $50,000 policy on the life of the other. If Tom dies, Joan collects $50,000 and can buy out Tom's share with a payment to his estate.

Budgeting

Spell out who pays for what budget items. Will rent be split fifty-fifty or proportionally based on the earnings of each? Will you split grocery bills regardless of your personal dietary habits? Who pays for dinners out? Contribute to a household petty cash envelope to cover groceries and other incidentals. If you share one phone number, each should pay his or her own long-distance charges.

Bank Accounts

In addition to individual checking accounts, some couples set up a joint account to cover shared household expenses, but it's generally not a good idea. There are too many sources of conflict. For example: If Partner A earns more than Partner B, should A subsidize B's rent or vacations or household expenses? If so, by how much? Will Partner A resent paying more than his or her equal share or feel entitled to more influence over how that money is spent? Will Partner B feel beholden to Partner A?

Certainly these sticky issues will have to be resolved whether or not the couple sets up a joint checking account. But keeping finances separate will help each partner retain financial independence, and that's worth the inconvenience of writing two checks to cover each household bill.

You want to avoid situations such as him criticizing the amount you spend on clothes or her criticizing the amount you spend on camera equipment. Save those fights for marriage!

Lease

Both names should be on the lease so there's no question you are jointly responsible for the rent.

Homeowner's Insurance

Renters must be covered under separate policies. If Partner A and Partner B own the house jointly, they can be covered under one policy that protects the property. If Partner A owns the house and Partner B moves in, Partner B could be added to A's policy. The reimbursement check to cover any losses, however, would be made out to Partner A, the policyholder. Therefore, to avoid any misunderstandings later, Partner B would be best protected under a separate tenant's policy in B's own name.

MARRIAGE

Ellen looked up from the guest list and frowned. "Don't get me wrong, Scott. I'm glad we're getting married. But why couldn't we elope? My mother is driving me crazy with these wedding plans."

"I don't see why you're getting so worked up about who sits where or whether there are lilies or violets on the tables," Scott replied. "Let your mother make these momentous decisions. Just relax."

"Relax? That's easy for you to say. You disappear into the library for ten hours a day and leave me to contend with seating charts and menus."

"I probably shouldn't mention this when you're in one of these moods, but my father asked me if we changed our legal and financial documents yet—our insurance policies and driver's licenses and all that."

"Your father was just looking for another opportunity to lament that I'm keeping my own last name," Ellen replied.

Many couples are so caught up in the minutia of planning a wedding that financial matters are obscured. Find time before walking down the aisle to resolve these points:

Premarital Agreements

As a prospective newlywed, probably the last thing you are contemplating is how to divide assets if the marriage ends. But it's important to think about, especially if one partner enters the marriage with substantially more assets than the other. In Ellen and Scott's case, neither is bringing enough material assets to the marriage to warrant the expense of drawing up a contract.

But couples should consider premarital contracts to clarify how joint assets would be divided if the marriage ends, to spell out who owns what, and to determine what portion of future earnings a working spouse is entitled to after supporting a partner during professional school. Without a premarital agreement, the laws of your state will determine how your property and assets will be divided should you divorce.

While a discussion of a marriage contract is enough to quell any romantic interlude, better to make agreements when you are happy than when you are bitterly contemplating divorce. If you didn't make a premarital agreement and would like to do so, it's not too late after the wedding—but it is unusual because the partner with more assets has less leverage after marriage in asking the other to sign.

Name Change

When a bride takes her husband's last name she must change her name on many documents. She must go to the local Social Security office with the marriage certificate to apply for a new card. She must also change her driver's license, insurance policies, and bank accounts. For a woman to maintain her credit history after changing her name, the name on the credit cards must be Jane Smith, not Mrs. Joseph Smith.

Resist the temptation to save annual fees on credit cards by getting a dependent's card on your husband's account. It's worth the $20 to $35 annual fee to maintain your credit identity should you become divorced or widowed. If you and your spouse combine surnames into one hyphenated name, that establishes separate credit identities for each. If you keep your maiden name, your credit identity remains intact.

Auto Insurance

Get one insurance policy that covers both if each of you has a car. By combining policies you will get a multiple car discount that reduces the overall rate by up to 25 percent. If you will be sharing a car formerly owned by one spouse, he or she should notify the insurer that there will be a secondary driver. Usually, there's no extra charge. If the car belonged to the wife and she changes her name or her residence, she must notify the insurer of the change. A change of residence is likely to affect the cost of the policy, especially if the move is from city to suburb (more expensive) or vice versa.

Life Insurance

If you have life insurance—including a term policy that is part of your employee benefits—you probably want to name your spouse as beneficiary. You may need to supplement your coverage if you just bought a house and meeting mortgage payments requires both incomes. Your options include buying enough insurance to replace the income of either partner, enough to pay off the mortgage in a lump sum, or buying special mortgage insurance that would pay off the mortgage loan if one spouse dies.

Health Insurance

If you must both have individual coverage from your employers and pay for premiums, it's probably cheaper to switch to family coverage on the better plan and drop the other. Another alternative is to keep both plans, name each other as dependents, and get more extensive coverage.

Homeowner's Insurance

If you move into a home owned by one of you before the marriage, no change is necessary because the policy is issued on the property, not the person who lives there. If you move into a home previously rented by one or both of you, consolidate renter's insurance policies.

Bank Accounts

You must decide whether you want separate or joint checking and savings accounts or a combination, which is the best idea. Keeping some money separate will help prevent fights.

If you choose a joint account, decide on one or two automated teller cards to access it. Two cards might create confusion unless each spouse keeps the other informed about withdrawals and deposits. Part of handling a joint account is working out an equitable record-keeping system. Do you want one spouse in charge or do you want to share duties? If one partner assumes the bulk of the responsibility, the other should know enough to take over in an emergency or a split-up. With a joint account, either partner has access to all the funds in the account, which could mean trouble if a couple separates on angry terms. A disadvantage to separate accounts is that if one spouse dies, the other doesn't have access to that account until the estate is settled. The money could be tied up for months or years.

Safe Deposit Box

If you each have your own safe deposit box, switch to one in both your names so each person has access to the contents, an important step if something happens to one partner.

Debts Brought to the Marriage

Decide if one partner will assume equal responsibility for paying off the other's debts. If one spouse has sizable debts, don't assume more debts as a couple, which could mean delaying the purchase of a home or other big items.

Equity Investments

Do you want a joint brokerage account? If so, you will need both signatures when you sell securities. Reassess your investment goals, which may change after marriage. For instance, if aggressive growth was your primary goal when single, you may want to switch to a more conservative strategy that combines growth and income.

Legal Documents

Naming your spouse as beneficiary if you already have a will, or a pension or profit-sharing plan is a simple matter. For the following items, however, seek legal advice:

- Both should draw up or update wills. If either of you dies without a will, the surviving spouse generally will receive only one-half to one-third of the estate, depending on state law. The rest will be divided among other relatives.
- Transferring property. You might want to transfer the title on real estate that you own individually to your joint names with "rights of survivorship," so when you die the property will pass automatically to your spouse without lengthy legal proceedings. Talk to your mortgage lender first to avoid breaching the mortgage agreement. You can transfer property to your spouse without paying a gift tax by using the marital gift deduction, a tax law provision that allows either spouse to give the other an unlimited amount.

PLANNING FOR CHILDREN

"I want a baby just as much as you do," Sue told Paul for perhaps the tenth time that week. "I'm just not sure we can afford one yet."

They seemed to have this conversation constantly, especially since Paul's brother and his wife had a baby two months before.

"We're not getting any younger," Paul reminded her. "You always said you wanted to have a baby by age thirty. It may take us a while to conceive."

"Paul, it's not going to take two years to get pregnant. You know what's holding me back. I'm not sure I'd want to go back to work right away and leave the baby with a stranger. And how will we afford a baby on half our income?"

"There's only one way to resolve this," Paul said. "Let's sit down and figure out the money involved."

Of course, having a child is not a financial decision like buying a house or a car. If everyone waited until they could definitely afford a child, many of us probably wouldn't be here. Still, it's wise to discuss and plan how to manage financially before a child is on the way.

How much will it cost? There's no magic formula to determine this, but you can be sure it will cost plenty. The daily living expenses for a baby's food, clothes, toiletries, and medical treatment will add at least $2,000 to $5,000 to your annual expenses, not including the costs of full-time child care or occasional babysitters. Add maternity clothes, nursery furniture and a layette, diapers, and bottles, and that can run another $2,000 to $3,000 before the baby's first birthday. If the pregnancy and delivery are routine, it will cost less than if a caesarian (a common complication) or other special medical treatment for the mother or baby is required. Fortunately for many couples, grandparents help out with the baby's expenses, and friends and relatives often pass down outgrown clothes, furniture, and toys. Yet, even with the most generous families and friends, expect a considerable cash outlay. And as children grow, so do their living expenses.

Figure the working mother's lost income as an expense of having a baby. For a woman earning $350 a week, before taxes, to stay at home for the first year would result in a $18,200 loss of family income. And the costs of returning to work don't always outweigh the benefits of the second income. For example, if that same mother paid $140 a week ($3.50 an hour for forty hours) for full-time child care, her take-home pay is reduced considerably. After subtracting the costs of commuting, a working wardrobe, and other business expenses, it may not pay to work. Your personal priorities weigh heavily in this equation: how you manage spending your days at home without a job or a paycheck, or, if you return to work, how you feel about leaving the baby with a sitter and determining how much time your husband can devote to child-care responsibilities.

Medical insurance will cover many childbirth costs, but your maternity benefits may not cover everything. Check that you changed your coverage after marriage from single to family with maternity benefits. Make sure you have coverage for both parents and the baby and that newborn nursery care is included. Find out if your policy pays a lump sum or a percentage of all costs (typically 80 percent), requiring you to pay the rest. If there are complications during the pregnancy or birth, will your policy pay all or some of the costs? For instance, your policy may cover only 50 percent of a caesarian birth.

When you are contemplating pregnancy, start building an emergency cash fund to cover unexpected expenses. Couples who are planning to live on one income should practice doing so for a while. You may discover you need more money than you expected. One spouse should explore the possibilities of part-time work or work that can be done from the home as a fallback or alternative to paying for full-time child care.

After working out income and budget projections, Sue and Paul came up with these figures: If Sue didn't return to work after her fully paid, eight-week maternity benefits expired, they would have about $1,500 a month to live on, after paying the mortgage and other fixed expenses, versus $3,000 if they both worked full-time. However, that $3,000 would be reduced by $600 for a baby-sitter, leaving $2,400 a month. The federal tax credit for child care would reduce this expense, but not by much, since the maximum credit for couples who earn more than a total of $28,000 is $480 a year for one child. (This is figured by the maximum of $2,400 in expenses multiplied by 20 percent.)

Money aside, Sue had doubts that she could leave the baby with a sitter while she worked full-time. "The best solution would be if I could work three days a week," Sue figured. "We could manage our expenses on 60 percent of my salary and I'd feel less guilty if I were home four days a week."

"What are the chances of that?" Paul asked.

"I think the company will be flexible because they don't want to lose me," Sue replied. "But let's think about the whole subject for a while. I don't want to be pressured into a decision."

Six months later, Sue was pregnant. She waited until her fourth month to inform her boss. He assured her that the company would let her work part-time for a year or so until she was ready to return full-time.

"Great. Everything's settled now," she told Paul happily. "I'm very relieved."

"Not everything," Paul reminded her. "We still have to change our insurance policies, revise our wills, and save more money."

"While you're worrying about the next twenty years, let me know when we can afford a bigger house. We're going to need it soon."

"Forget it," Paul replied. "We can't afford a bigger mortgage on a smaller income. And our house is big enough. Besides, we have to start saving for college tuition."

When a child is on the way, take these steps to plan for the future:

1. Revise your wills. If you never got around to drawing up wills, do it now for your and for the child's sake. Choose guardians for your child and name a trustee to manage the child's finances.
2. Increase your insurance coverage. Your liability and life insurance needs escalate with the birth of a child. Increase your homeowner's liability coverage to at least $100,000. You will be exposed to more risks: Your child may be hurt in an accident or cause one.

   You need more life insurance coverage to provide for your child's education, and survivorship income, in case either or both of you die. If one spouse stops working to rear children, then you must provide survivorship benefits to her or him as well.

   One suggestion: You can set up a **trust** funded by a $250,000 term insurance policy on the husband's life, assuming he is the primary earner, for about $300 a year. If the husband dies, the trust will pay the wife a $25,000 annuity and provide education money for any children when they turn 18.

3. Make sure you have a cash savings cushion equal to the sum of the deductibles on all your insurance policies.
4. Redo the family budget. Allot at least $2,000 a year for the baby's expenses, which probably means cutting back or eliminating travel, clothing, and entertainment. Saving for a bigger home, if that's a priority, must be reflected in the budget, too.
5. Finance college costs. Yes, you should start planning eighteen years in advance. Saving $50 a month per child for eighteen years should provide you with $13,000 to $15,000 in today's dollars—enough for one to two years of private school or maybe four years at a state school.
6. With the help of your accountant, lawyer, or financial planner, examine methods of shifting income from you to your child by setting up trusts and establishing custodial accounts.

For example, you can open a bank account in your child's name under the Uniform Gift to Minors Act. You can give up to $10,000 a year, or $20,000 from both parents, tax-free. Your child can collect $1,100 in income and dividends per year without paying any taxes; the rest is taxed at the child's tax rate, presumably lower than yours.

One disadvantage to custodial accounts is that you can't take back the money after your child turns eighteen. If your son or daughter grows up to be a rock singer and wants to spend the money on leather and sequined clothes rather than college tuition, there's nothing you can do. To avoid this, enlist your lawyer to set up a trust—such as a Clifford trust—that returns the assets to your control after a certain time period.

Another warning: When you give money to your child or set up a trust, you usually can't use the income from the account to pay for expenses you are legally required to provide, such as food, clothing, and shelter.

7. Plan your taxes. Claiming your child as a dependent means you may deduct $1,000 from your taxable income. There's no limit to the number of dependents you may have. And as long as you pay someone else to care for your child while you work, you can take the child-care credit. Unlike the dependency deduction, the credit is a dollar-for-dollar subtraction from taxes that you would otherwise owe. The credit is available to couples who both work full-time, part-time, or are actively seeking work, or when one parent works part-time and the other is a full-time student or disabled.

The credit is worth 20 to 30 percent of the first $2,400 in outlays for the care of one child and the first $4,800 spent for the care of two or more. If you and your spouse earn a combined income over $28,000, the maximum credit is $480 for one child and $960 for two or more children. There is a hitch: The credit is limited by the earnings of the lower-paid spouse. Thus, if one spouse's income is less than $2,400, with one child, the couple couldn't receive the maximum credit.

APPENDIX I:
Formula for Figuring Yield to Maturity on a Bond

Here is an approximate formula for calculating yield to maturity—the rate of return on a bond held to redemption. As an example, consider a bond selling for $800 with a face value of $1,000, paying annual interest of $100 with a redemption in five years.

1. First subtract the selling price from the face value.
   $1,000 minus $800 equals $200.
2. Divide the difference by the number of years to redemption.
   $200 divided by 5 equals $40
3. Add the interest payment.
   $40 plus $100 equals $140
4. Divide by the average of the selling price and the face value.
   $140 divided by $$\frac{\$800 \text{ plus } \$1,000}{2}$$
   or
   $140 divided by $900 equals 15.6 percent.
Therefore, 15.6 percent is the yield to maturity.

APPENDIX II:

Best Performing Mutual Funds over Fifteen Years, Ten Years, Five Years, and One Year

(Source: Lipper Analytical Services, New York)

Fifteen Years: 12/31/69 to 12/31/84

Fund	Percent Gain from Amount Invested
1. International Investors	1209.14%
2. Fidelity Magellan Fund	1056.75
3. Templeton Growth	956.62
4. Twentieth Century Select	955.64
5. Mutual Shares Corporation	950.74
6. Pioneer II	876.89
7. Twentieth Century Growth	740.59
8. Over-the-Counter Securities	664.35
9. Fidelity Equity-Income	616.86
10. Quasar Associates	607.21
11. Weingarten Equity	589.55
12. Charter Fund	551.44
13. FPA Paramount	548.74
14. Windsor Fund	548.38
15. American Capital Comstock	544.36

Ten Years: 12/31/74 to 12/31/84

1. Fidelity Magellan Fund	1784.27%
2. Pennsylvania Mutual	1476.19
3. Lindner Fund	1342.08
4. Evergreen Fund	1274.52
5. Twentieth Century Growth	1222.63
6. Twentieth Century Select	1194.06

7.	American Capital Venture	1158.00
8.	Sequoia Fund	1148.57
9.	Oppenheimer Special	1097.94
10.	American Capital Pace	1090.44
11.	Quasar Associates	1049.42
12.	Value Line Leveraged Growth	982.08
13.	Fidelity Destiny	941.34
14.	Sigma Venture Shares	931.56
15.	American Capital Comstock	926.72

Five Years: 12/31/79 to 12/31/84

1.	Fidelity Magellan Fund	314.22%
2.	Lindner Dividend	246.74
3.	Lindner Fund	219.83
4.	Vanguard Qualified Dividend-1	213.76
5.	Phoenix Stock	213.28
6.	Phoenix Growth	201.46
7.	American Capital Pace	200.64
8.	United Vanguard Fund	189.93
9.	New England Life Growth	185.37
10.	Loomis-Sayles Capital	182.92
11.	Lehman Capital Fund	181.13
12.	Fidelity Equity-Income	178.35
13.	Nicholas Fund	172.43
14.	Windsor Fund	170.99
15.	Sequoia Fund	170.85

One Year: 12/31/83 to 12/31/84

1.	Prudential Bache Utility	38.62%
2.	Vanguard Qualified Dividend-1	25.59
3.	Copley Tax-Managed	23.93
4.	American Telecommunications-Income	22.26
5.	Franklin Utilities	21.42

6. Energy & Utilities Shares	21.19
7. Fidelity Select Utilities	20.87
8. Fidelity Qualified Dividend	20.86
9. Windsor Fund	19.57
10. Sequoia Fund	18.55
11. General Electric LT Interest	18.51
12. Composite Income Fund	18.21
13. Fidelity Select Financial	17.99
14. ABT Utility Income Fund	17.30
15. Nicholas II	16.92

APPENDIX III:

Addresses of IRS Service Centers

Alabama—Atlanta, GA
31101
Alaska—Ogden, UT 84201
Arizona—Ogden, UT 84201
Arkansas—Austin, TX 73301
California—Fresno, CA
93888
Colorado—Ogden, UT
84201
Connecticut—Andover, MA
05501
Delaware—Philadelphia, PA
19255
District of Columbia—
Philadelphia, PA 19255
Florida—Atlanta, GA 31101
Georgia—Atlanta, GA 31101
Hawaii—Fresno, CA 93888
Idaho—Ogden, UT 84201
Illinois—Kansas City, MO
64999
Indiana—Memphis, TN
37501
Iowa—Kansas City, MO
64999
Kansas—Austin, TX 73301
Kentucky—Memphis, TN
37501
Louisiana—Austin, TX 73301
Maine—Andover, MA 05501
Maryland—Philadelphia, PA
19255
Massachusetts—Andover, MA
05501

Michigan—Cincinnati, OH
45999
Minnesota—Ogden, UT
84201
Mississippi—Atlanta, GA
31101
Missouri—Kansas City, MO
64999
Montana—Ogden, UT 84201
Nebraska—Ogden, UT
84201
Nevada—Ogden, UT 84201
New Hampshire—Andover,
MA 05501
New Jersey—Holtsville, NY
00501
New Mexico—Austin, TX
73301
New York—*New York City
and Counties of Nassau,
Rockland, Suffolk and
Westchester*—
Holtsville, NY
00501
All Other Counties—
Andover, MA
05501
North Carolina—Memphis,
TN 37501
North Dakota—Ogden, UT
84201
Ohio—Cincinnati, OH 45999
Oklahoma—Austin, TX
73301

Oregon—Ogden, UT 84201
Pennsylvania—Philadelphia,
PA 19255
Rhode Island—Andover, MA
05501
South Carolina—Atlanta, GA
31101
South Dakota—Ogden, UT
84201
Tennessee—Memphis, TN
37501
Texas—Austin, TX 73301
Utah—Ogden, UT 84201
Vermont—Andover, MA
05501
Virginia—Memphis, TN
37501
Washington—Ogden, UT
84201
West Virginia—Memphis,
TN 37501
Wisconsin—Kansas City, MO
64999

Wyoming—Ogden, UT
84201
American Samoa—
Philadelphia, PA 19255
Guam—Commissioner of
Revenue and Taxation,
Agana, GU 96910
Puerto Rico (or if excluding
income under section 933)
—Philadelphia, PA
19255
Virgin Island:
Non-permanent residents
—Philadelphia, PA
19255
Permanent residents—
Bureau of Internal
Revenue, Charlotte
Amalie, St. Thomas, VI
00801

APPENDIX IV:
Tax-Free Equivalent Table

Single Return*		$28.8 to $34.1	$34.1 to $41.5	$41.5 to $55.3		$55.3 to $81.8		Over $81.8
Joint Return*			$45.8 to $60.0	$60.0 to $85.6	$85.6 to $109.4		$109.4 to $162.4	Over $162.4
1984 Tax Bracket		34%	38%	42%	45%	48%	49%	50%
	4.00	6.06	6.45	6.90	7.27	7.69	7.84	8.00
	4.50	6.82	7.26	7.76	8.18	8.65	8.82	9.00
	5.00	7.58	8.06	8.62	9.09	9.62	9.80	10.00
	5.50	8.33	8.87	9.48	10.00	10.58	10.78	11.00
	6.00	9.09	9.68	10.34	10.91	11.54	11.76	12.00
	6.50	9.85	10.48	11.21	11.82	12.50	12.75	13.00
	7.00	10.61	11.29	12.07	12.73	13.46	13.73	14.00
Tax-	7.50	11.36	12.10	12.93	13.64	14.42	14.71	15.00
Exempt	8.00	12.12	12.90	13.79	14.55	15.38	15.69	16.00
Yields	8.50	12.88	13.71	14.66	15.45	16.35	16.67	17.00
(%)	9.00	13.64	14.52	15.52	16.36	17.31	17.65	18.00
	9.50	14.39	15.32	16.38	17.27	18.27	18.63	19.00
	10.00	15.15	16.13	17.24	18.18	19.23	19.61	20.00
	10.50	15.91	16.94	18.10	19.09	20.19	20.59	21.00
	11.00	16.67	17.74	18.97	20.00	21.15	21.57	22.00
	11.50	17.42	18.55	19.83	20.91	22.12	22.55	23.00
	12.00	18.18	19.35	20.69	21.82	23.08	23.53	24.00

*Net amount subject to federal income tax after deductions and exemptions.

BIBLIOGRAPHY

This book covers the basics. For supplementary reading, here is a list divided by topics:

General Personal Finance

Hallman, Victor G., and Rosenbloom, Jerry S. *Personal Financial Planning.* 3rd ed., revised. New York: McGraw-Hill, 1983. $27.50.

Phillips, Carol. *Money Talk: The Last Taboo.* New York: Arbor House, 1984. $15.95.

Siverd, Bonnie. *Count Your Change: A Woman's Guide to Sudden Financial Change.* New York: Arbor House, 1983. $6.95, paper.

Weinstein, Grace W. *The Lifetime Book of Money Management.* New York: New American Library, 1984. $19.50.

Taxes

Andersen, Arthur, & Co. *Tax Shelters: The Basics.* New York: Harper & Row, 1983. $13.95.

Block, Julian. *Julian Block's Guide to Year-Round Tax Savings.* New York: Dow-Jones Irwin, 1985. $9.95, paper.

IRS publication 17. *Your Federal Income Tax.* Free from the IRS.

Lasser, J.K. *Your Income Tax.* 1985 ed. New York: Simon & Schuster, 1985. $6.95

Sprouse, Mary L. *Taxable You: Every Woman's Guide to Taxes.* New York: Penguin Books, 1984. $8.95, paper.

Insurance

Golonka, Nancy. *How to Protect What's Yours.* London: Acropolis Books, Ltd., 1983. $6.95, paper.

Hunt, James H. *Taking the Bite Out of Insurance: How to Save Money on Life Insurance.* Alexandria, VA.: National Insurance Consumer Organization, 344 Commerce Street, 22314, 1984. $7.25.

Mink, Stephen. *Insuring Your Home.* New York: Congdon & Weed, 1984. $13.95.

Tobias, Andrew. *The Invisible Bankers.* New York: Pocket Books, 1983. $3.95, paper.

Credit
Stribling, Catherine. *Getting the Most From Your Bank.* New York: Ballantine, 1984. $2.95, paper.

Investments
Donoghue, William, with Tilling, Thomas. *William Donoghue's No-Load Mutual Fund Guide.* New York: Bantam, 1985. $3.95, paper.

Dreman, David. *The New Contrarian Investment Strategy.* New York: Random House, 1983. $16.95.

Engel, Louis, and Boyd, Brendan. *How to Buy Stocks.* New York: Bantam, 1984. $3.95, paper.

Graham, Benjamin. *The Intelligent Investor.* New York: Harper & Row, 1973. $16.50.

Hardy, Colburn C. *Dun & Bradstreet's Guide to Your Investments 1985.* 30th ed. New York: Harper & Row, 1985. $9.95, paper.

Nelson, Wayne F. *How to Buy Money.* New York: McGraw-Hill, 1982. $5.95, paper.

Tobias, Andrew. *The Only Investment Guide You'll Ever Need.* New York: Bantam, 1983. $3.95, paper.

Train, John. *Preserving Capital and Making It Grow.* New York: Penguin Books, 1984. $8.95, paper.

Real Estate
Blumberg, Richard E., and Grow, James R. *The Rights of Tenants: The Basic American Civil Liberties Union Guide to a Tenant's Rights.* New York: Avon, 1978. $3.95, paper.

Boroson, Wayne. *How to Buy or Sell Your Home in a Changing Market.* Brooklyn, N.Y.: Medical Economics Books, Box C779 Pratt Street, 11201, 1983. $15.95 plus $1.50 handling.

Goldstick, David T., and Janik, Carolyn. *The Complete Guide to Co-ops and Condominiums.* New York: New American Library, 1983. $7.95, paper.

Miller, Peter G. *The Common Sense Mortgage: How to Cut the Cost of Home Ownership by $100,000 or More.* New York, Harper & Row, 1984. $12.45.

Nessen, Robert. *The Real Estate Book.* New York: Signet, 1983. $3.95, paper.

Sumichrast, Michael, and Shafer, Ronald G. *The Complete Book of Home Buying.* New York: Bantam, 1982. $3.95, paper.

Turner, R. J. *A Consumer's Guide to the Mortgage Maze.* 1st ed. New York: St. Martin's Press, 1983. $14.95.

Retirement

Grace, William J., Jr. *The ABCs of IRAs.* New York: Dell, 1984. $4.95.

Krughoff, Robert, and the Center for the Studies of Services. *The IRA Book.* Washington, D.C.: The Center for the Studies of Services (1518 K Street, NW, Suite 406, 20005), 1984. $6.95, paper.

GLOSSARY

Adjustable rate mortgage (ARM). A mortgage with an interest rate that moves up or down according to an economic index.

Annuity. A contract with an insurance company in which you pay a certain amount of money and in return are paid a periodic income for a specified time or for life.

Appreciation. An increase in value.

Assets. Everything you own or is due to you, such as cash and investments.

Basis (of property value). A figure computed by adding the cost of improvements to the original cost of a property; used for tax purposes.

Bear market. The stock market when it is declining in value. A bear is a person who believes the market will decline.

Bond. A loan to a corporation or municipality. The holder of the bond is guaranteed a rate of interest for a specific time period.

Broker. A person who negotiates sales of securities and commodities for the public in return for a commission.

Bull market. The stock market when it is appreciating in value. A bull is a person who believes the market will rise.

Capital gain. Profits realized from the sale of a security or real estate. A capital gain acquired in less than six months is short-term and taxed at the federal income tax rate; a long-term capital gain on an asset held for more than six months is subject to a lower tax rate of 40 percent of the income tax rate.

Capital loss. The loss realized from the sale of an asset such as a security or real estate, which is tax deductible to some extent.

Certificates of Deposit (CDs). Savings, usually in units of $1,000, deposited in a bank or savings and loan institution for a specific time period in return for a guaranteed interest rate.

Churning. Excessive transactions netting your stockbroker more in commissions than you receive in profits.

Closing costs. The expenses such as lawyers' fees that must be paid above the price of a property before a title is transferred.

Conventional mortgage. A mortgage that has a fixed interest rate and a fixed time period.

Creative financing. Novel ways for a buyer to finance the purchase of property, often involving assistance from the seller.

Credit (for tax). A dollar-for-dollar offset against the tax you would otherwise owe. Regardless of your tax bracket, a $100 credit would reduce your tax liability by $100.

Deduction (for tax). A reduction on the amount of income on which you figure your taxes. The savings from a deduction depends on your tax bracket; the higher the bracket, the more you save.

Depreciation (for tax). A periodic deduction for part of the original cost of an asset or property over its estimated useful life. If a building is worth $60,000 and its useful life is 30 years, the owner could depreciate $2,000 a year ($60,000 divided by 30 years).

Diversification. Spreading investment dollars among different types of investments to reduce the chance of a catastrophic loss.

Dividends. A payment distributed to shareholders.

Endorsement (or rider). A form attached to an insurance policy to add or alter its original provisions, spelling out what is and isn't covered.

Equity. Your claim or share of an asset. The equity you have in your home is the value of the house reduced by the outstanding amount of the mortgage.

Escrow. Money and documents related to a transaction that are placed in the custody of a third party until certain conditions are met.

FDIC (Federal Deposit Insurance Company). The government agency that guarantees funds up to $100,000 at member banks.

Float. The time it takes a check you've written to clear your bank and be deducted from your account.

FSLIC (Federal Savings and Loan Insurance Corporation). The government agency that insures funds on deposit at member savings and loan associations.

Fundamental research and analysis. Evaluating a company's prospects based on a variety of economic factors such as its sales, assets, earning potential, products, markets, and management.

Income averaging. A method for computing taxes which allows you to figure the tax on part of your income as if you received it in equal slices over a four-year period rather than in one year. Your taxes are reduced because some of your income can be taxed in a lower bracket than normal.

Individual Retirement Account (IRA). A retirement plan that allows individuals with earned income to defer taxes on $2,000 a year (or $2,250 for a couple with one nonworking spouse). An IRA is a shelter for investments in stocks, bonds, mutual funds, bank accounts, and other financial products.

Interest. The rent a borrower pays for the use of money. Simple interest is computed on the original sum invested; compound interest is paid on both the principal sum invested and on accumulated interest.

KEOGH plan. A retirement plan for self-employed people and their employees, which in most cases allows them to defer taxes on $30,000 or *20 percent* of net earnings annually, whichever is less.

Liabilities. Claims or debts held against an individual or a corporation.

Lien. A legal claim on a property as payment of or security for a debt.

Load. A sales charge in a mutual fund, deducted from the investment so that not all your savings are invested. A typical load is 8.5 percent. A low-load is a sales charge of 1 percent to 3 percent. With a no-load fund there is no sales charge.

Marginal tax bracket. The percentage of every dollar the government takes above a certain income level.

Maturity. The date when a loan or bond becomes due and payable to the holder.

Money market mutual fund. An investment company or mutual fund that invests in short-term money instruments such as bank certificates of deposit, short-term government securities, and commercial paper.

Mortgage. A loan to be repaid with interest and secured with a pledge of real property.

Municipal or tax-exempt bond. A bond issued by a state or local government. The interest on it is exempt from federal income taxes, and also from state and local income taxes within the state it is issued.

Mutual fund. A company that invests in securities of other corporations. Fund managers buy and sell securities, combining the money of many investors. Individuals buy shares of the fund, which fluctuate in value daily based on the value of the underlying securities.

Net worth. All your assets minus all your liabilities.

New issues. Stock offerings designed to provide capital for the expansion of small companies. The new money usually goes to boost working capital, expand products and markets, and retire debt.

Note. A written statement that acknowledges a debt and promises payment.

Odd lot. To buy fewer than the standard trading block (which is called a round lot). Common stocks and corporate and municipal bonds trade in round lots of 100.

Personal articles floater. A supplement to your basic insurance policy to cover specific items such as jewelry or other valuables.

Points. The fee charged by the lending institution for giving a mortgage or loan. One point is equal to 1 percent of the amount of the loan.

Portfolio. Your total investment holdings.

Price/earnings (P/E) ratio. The price of a share of common stock divided by its earnings per share for the past year. For example, a stock selling for $25 per share and earning $5 per share is trading at a p/e ratio of five to one.

Prospectus. The official booklet that describes an investment and offers its shares for sale. It contains such information as investment objectives, policies, services, fees, and how shares can be bought and sold.

Rally. A rise in price of the general market or a particuliar security.

SBIC (Savings Bank Life Insurance). Life insurance policies sold over-the-counter to residents of Connecticut, New York, and Massachusetts. There are no commissions or fees to agents, which keeps prices down, but each state limits the amount individuals may buy: up to $25,000 in Connecticut, $30,000 in New York, and $62,000 in Massachusetts, so it's best for people who don't need much coverage.

Second trust. A loan secured by your property—but any claim on the property is second in line to the claim by a party with an existing secured loan.

Securities. A general term for stocks, bonds, and other investments.

Stock. Shares of ownership in a company. There are two kinds: common has no fixed, guaranteed dividend; preferred will pay a predetermined dividend as long as the company stays solvent.

Tax shelter. An arrangement that allows you to legally eliminate, reduce, or postpone the amount you must pay in taxes.

Some shelters are scams set up by fraudulent promoters and the IRS is on the lookout for them.

Technical research and analysis. A method of evaluating a stock by studying the patterns and trends of it's price.

Term insurance. Pure life insurance, without a savings component, which allows you to buy a specified amount of protection for a specified time period.

Treasury bills (T-bills). Short-term U.S. government obligations issued for periods of one year or less. They are issued at auction for a $10,000 minimum and the proceeds are used to finance the government's daily operations.

Treasury bonds. U.S. government obligations issued for periods of five to thirty years.

Treasury notes. U.S. government obligations issued for periods of more than one year but less than five years.

Trust. A legal arrangement that allows property or money to be put aside and managed by a trustee for a beneficiary.

Unit trust. A portfolio of specific bonds. An investor may buy a certain number of shares or units of each portfolio. The units can be bought and sold in the secondary market and are maintained by the brokerage firm that assembled the trust.

Universal life insurance. A variation of whole life insurance that combines elements of term life insurance and a tax-deferred savings plan.

Whole life (also called **ordinary** or **straight life**) **insurance.** An insurance policy with a savings or cash value that increases every year. You pay the same amount of premium each year.

Yield (or return). Income (dividends or interest) expressed as a percentage of the current price. A stock selling at $20 with a dividend of $2 per share would yield 10 percent.

Zero bracket amount. The built-in deduction the government gives to non-itemizers to offset income on their tax returns. It used to be called the standard deduction.

INDEX